It's a WILD Life

How My Life Became a Zoo

BUD DeYOUNG

with
Cindy Martinusen Coloma

It's a WILD Life

How My Life Became a Zoo

BUD DeYOUNG

with
Cindy Martinusen Coloma

MEDALLION
P R E S S

Medallion Press, Inc.

Printed in USA

To my mother, Rosemary, for encouraging me when I was young to pursue my love for wildlife and always pushing me to pursue my dreams. You are the best mom anyone could wish to have. I love you, Mom!

Published 2014 by Medallion Press, Inc.

The MEDALLION PRESS LOGO
is a registered trademark of Medallion Press, Inc.

Copyright © 2014 by Bud DeYoung and Cindy Martinusen Coloma
Cover design by James Tampa
Edited by Lorie Popp Jones
Interior photos supplied and printed with permission from the DeYoung family
Photos on pages VII, XII, 6, 87, 105, 154, 160, 181, 190, 200, 203, 204, 234, 250, 252, 254, 256 by James Tampa

Cataloging-in-Publication Data is on file with the Library of Congress.

Typeset in Georgia
Printed in the United States of America

ISBN 978-160542-637-2

10 9 8 7 6 5 4 3 2 1
First Edition

ACKNOWLEDGMENTS

A special thanks to Carrie Cramer, my love. You have always backed me. Your passion and dedication made my zoo grow to where it is today and helped guide me through writing this book.

Thank you, Cindy Coloma, for putting my words, my life, into a book. You are a talented writer.

And thank you to all the wonderful people and animal lovers who have always supported and continue to support my zoo.

—Bud DeYoung

An enormous thanks to my mom and grandma, Gail McCormick and Ruby Duvall, for enormous amounts of help on this project from transcribing to babysitting. And I can't forget "Papa" too! I truly couldn't have completed this without you.

My husband, children, sister, parents, all my family and friends are such a support and source of inspiration. I can't thank you enough, and it would be pages to do so here.

My editors at Medallion, Emily Steele and Lorie Jones, were wonderful to work with. Emily, I greatly appreciated your encouragement and guidance along the journey, and it was a pleasure getting to know you. Lorie, your line edits were excellent as always, and it's always a gift to be around you.

Through the process of writing this book with Bud DeYoung, I was so impressed and amazed at Bud's and Carrie's love, sacrifice, and devotion to animals of every kind. These people give their hearts and lives to every one, whether a chicken or a hippo. It was unlike anything I've ever seen. I wish for them great blessings, hordes of volunteers, and financial support to no end—as you deserve in your quest to save animals and give people a new understanding of both the domestic and wild kingdoms. Oh, and some milder winters would be nice too. Bud and Carrie, you have my unending admiration. Thank you for welcoming me into your crazy lives—it was an honor.

—Cindy Martinusen Coloma

Carrie and Bud taking animals out for an educational talk at the zoo.

CONTENTS

PART ONE
The Passion

Carrie and Bud spending time outside with Louie the chimp.

CHAPTER ONE
Early Rising

I wake to animals.

This morning, it's a chimp crawling on my head.

I've never been one to linger in bed, but two-year-old orphan Louie is an insistent alarm clock and makes slow waking impossible. He stretches out my ears, tugs the bit of short-cropped hair I have left, and if I wait much longer, he'll dump everything from the dressers onto the floor.

I can't remember a time when a baby hyena, wolf, bear cub, monkey, or other exotic creature didn't share my bed. My fiancée, Carrie, and I have had eight years of animal housemates. Before that, my years can be marked by my children growing up and the myriad of animals passing through the doors of the house and the habitats all over my land.

It's still before dawn. Carrie's already gone, the bed cold on her side. Two horses came in late to her rescue ranch. They were in bad shape from malnutrition and abuse. She'll be tending to them day and night between everything else. Last year she saved two Clydesdales that were shot by their owner and left for weeks to rot and die. The calls for help come in daily, and neither of us knows how to manage everything or to say no.

Now that I think about it, I wonder if Carrie ever made it to bed at all.

The cost of feed tugs at my thoughts as much as Louie's strong fingers prying at my mouth. I kick off the covers, and Louie jumps, cheering. He climbs up my aching back onto my shoulders.

"Let's get you some breakfast," I say and give him a friendly rub on the arm.

Quite literally, my life is a zoo. For the past forty-odd years, I've built the DeYoung Family Zoo in Wallace, Michigan, on first forty, now sixty acres surrounding this eight-hundred-square-foot house constructed in 1979.

In the past few years, Carrie launched her no-kill Piper's Rescue Ranch. It's located on leased land adjacent to mine that might soon be sold out from under her. The rescue grew out of the zoo, from people bringing pets they didn't want or couldn't care for any longer. We've taken in chickens, turtles, iguanas . . . You name it—we've probably had it.

After the coffee is set to brew, Louie pounds my shoulder as I make his bottle. I focus on the day ahead. I thank God it's busy this month. August has brought us more visitors. Those visitors get me out of bed, bones creaking and an ache in my back. I love introducing people to animals of every kind. I want them to get close, learn something new, and leave with a fresh appreciation for the animal kingdom. That's why I started the zoo, or maybe the animals started it all.

The busy month is a bit of hope after a horrendous July when a heat wave kept the visitors away. We dropped behind forty-four thousand dollars in one month. That's money to get us through the coming winter. Not only Carrie and me but four hundred hungry animals at the zoo and the ones Carrie's harboring at the rescue—I reckon it's at least several hundred and growing.

I cradle Louie in my arms as he slurps down his bottle. I glance around at the other animals. The dogs are out, so Carrie was here. The babies in their pens will eat soon when our summer volunteer comes in for morning feeding. In the spring, we have babies to feed every three hours and often with no help, but this time of year, our good-hearted friends and neighbors spend their mornings and sometimes all day helping around both places. We'll soon be losing the high school and college helpers as summer winds down. Then winter shuts us in, and we're on our own again.

"Let's get moving," I say to the chimp when he sucks only air through the bottle.

Louie stares up at me, studying my face. He looks to

Carrie and me as surrogate parents. It won't be like this forever. Though it's incredibly similar to having a new baby and now a toddler in the house, chimpanzees aren't humans and they aren't pets. There'll come a time when Louie will move to his own primate habitat with siblings and perhaps a mate.

But I'm not thinking of that right now with too much looming ahead. I have morning feedings, a dead cow to pick up from a local farm, food for the big cats, hay and a few groceries to grab in town, a farmhand who volunteered but needs a ride, and a dozen other chores waiting before the zoo gates open at 10:00 a.m.

My phone buzzes with a text from Carrie.

Morning, Caveman. Belle and Chance have gained pounds already. I'm worried the donkey might have foundered, though. Vet at 8:00 a.m. Three new dogs coming in this afternoon. I'll get them after the Big Cat Feeding. See you at 1:00 p.m.

I tap at the keys worse than Louie can do. Technology and I don't get along, but who can deny its convenience? I want to tell Carrie not to worry, but I can't think of any good words. I'll call her later, I decide, and pour a cup of coffee to go. Louie finds his place on my shoulder.

The day beckons or, more accurately, the hundreds of animals waiting for their morning feed. The bears whine when they see me through the kitchen window, the tigers yawn, and the wolves sniff the air as they hear the door

BUD DeYOUNG

creak open, even from their habitats all over the park.

As I head out, most people are still warm in their beds. Once in a while, I wonder what it's like for folks who have the luxury of waking up good and slow. Guess they'd never find it a luxury to hear the coffee brewing and smell its aroma from beneath the covers.

I walk into a cool morning in the Upper Peninsula, with chickens clucking, a cow mooing, and a lion off in the distance letting out a roar.

Truth be told, I wouldn't have life any other way.

Louie loves going for a ride on the ATV as we patrol the park as part of our daily routine.

CHAPTER TWO
The Call of the Wild

The morning sun cuts low through the thick pines as I maneuver the four-wheeler along the gravel trails crisscrossing sixty acres of animal habitats. This early breeze cools my face as I rise up to check animals and fencing with my beige DeYoung Family Zoo shirt flapping in the wind. The animals are awake, enjoying this time before the August heat beats down upon us.

As I ride the trail toward Wallace, our gray African hippopotamus, I know he's waiting. He sits in his pond with only his ears, eyes, and the top of his nose protruding from the water. Once he hears the four-wheeler, Wallace's ears pop up, and he moves toward the ramp. I know this because I've spied on him to watch his reactions. Wallace can't see the road beyond the walls of his pond, but he's always waiting when I run up that ramp.

"Hi there, Wallace," I yell. "Are you hungry?"

Wallace moves his three-thousand-pound body, dancing

back and forth and making a woo-woo-woo sound.

I reach out to rub the end of his smooth nose and put a head of romaine in his mouth.

Wallace follows my voice. I don't use gesture commands but just talk to him. If I say, "Wallace, open," he opens his mouth. We've spent so much time together that he has a good idea what I'm asking.

Later this afternoon, I'll demonstrate this to our visitors and also how Wallace can crush a watermelon like a grape with his powerful jaws. That always amazes them.

But this morning before the crowds, the exclamations of intrigue, and the bombarding of questions, it's just my animals and me. I savor these moments, though I probably enjoy sharing my critters with visitors as much as I like my time alone with them. Each one has such unique characteristics and qualities that I want to share them. I guess that hasn't changed much since I first started raising animals as a little boy.

The path from my childhood in a suburban home in Highland, Indiana, to this rural private zoo in the Upper Peninsula of Michigan is paved with animal memories.

It probably started with a flock of ducks. Or it might have been my first dog, Barney the Saint Bernard. Barney was a fabulous childhood pal, towering larger than life. There was also the squirrel monkey I brought home after exchanging it for our beagle. What kid could turn down that trade?

My father and I in 1955. Birthday time at my grandma's house. I treasure the memories of my father.

I was born in 1953, the oldest of four children. Our home in Highland sat on a neatly paved street with side-walks and scrunched-up houses separated by fenced yards. Maybe ideal for *Leave It to Beaver* but not the best location for a backyard farm.

My parents owned a garden center and a grocery store. When I was eight years old, I started trimming lettuce, cutting celery, and working in the garden center. I knew every plant, tree, and shrub. My younger brother, Randy, followed a few years behind. It was a family business, and we didn't mind helping out.

Early on, I learned how to work hard and that it got me money in return. This was so far back that the vending machines had Mountain Dew in green glass bottles with a little hillbilly on the label. One bottle cost a dime. Gasoline was seventeen cents a gallon.

My mom and dad weren't well-to-do, but they were loved by everyone and they worked really hard. I remember work, work, work, from daylight to dark. Even years later, when my dad was dying from colon cancer and went blind from diabetes, he still went to the grocery store when he wasn't in the hospital. He'd paint the signs and feel his way around. He was an admirable father, and I loved him a lot.

Long before he got sick, my dad took me out to a farm in Crown Point, Indiana. This place had all kinds of poultry—pheasants, chickens, and turkeys. At eight or nine years old, I wanted to live on that farm. My parents wanted to get out of the suburbs as well, but plans for that move were far down the road.

But Dad let me bring home a little flock of ducks. I made a pool in the backyard and loved feeding and watching the ducks. Then I added chickens and pigeons while building an animal rescue operation. I constructed cages for birds with broken wings and for pigeons that followed breadcrumbs into my traps.

From childhood into my teenage years, my life revolved around working at my dad's stores and caring for the various animals I had in the backyard. I wasn't like the other kids in my neighborhood who played sports at the park, collected baseball cards, and went to the movies. I had fire-engine red hair, something I inevitably was teased about, but those kids liked coming to see my little backyard zoo. I charged a quarter for the entrance fee and a guided tour. They didn't come back to play, but I didn't have a need for that.

When I was around fifteen, this gentleman came into the grocery store to pick up produce and lettuce scraps like many people did at that time. We started talking and made introductions, and he told me the produce trimmings were for his backyard collection of geese, pigeons, and other kinds of birds. Little did I know, this encounter with George Dragic from Griffith, Indiana, would bring me a mentor and friend who would help shape the course of my life.

"I'd like to come out and see what you have," I told him.

George invited me to do just that.

"How about tomorrow?" I asked, figuring out how I'd squeeze in a trip after work.

The next day, I rode my bicycle seven miles to his place. I was really good at biking at that time.

George was a machinist by trade. He also dealt in scrap metal and wire around Gary, Indiana. He bought second-hand wire for small animal cages and then sold it at bird shows and to breeders. He also raised goats that he sold and traded along with some sheep.

It wasn't hard to see my interest in the birds. George sent me home with some homing pigeons, and I was hooked.

George invited my brother and me on his next haul down to St. John, Indiana, for a livestock sale. Randy and I were young and strong: good help for George, who was in his sixties. After that, we started going with George to pigeon shows, livestock sales, and all kinds of places that centered around animals.

Randy raised powder pigeons, and I raised Birmingham Rollers and homing pigeons. We joined the Munster and Highland Pigeon Club. In our backyard, we built two different coops, where we competed over who had the best pigeons. We entered pigeon shows to see who got the best ribbons.

But more than the competition, I developed a deep love for pigeons: witnessing them hatch, seeing them raise the little squabs, and watching them fly. To this day, I still love chickens and pigeons as much as my bears and tigers. Whenever Carrie goes on zoo business out of town, she always brings me back a new breed of bird as a gift.

One afternoon as I pulled up on my bike after school, I saw a squad car leaving the house. My mom said a neighbor complained that pigeons were landing on her roof, ducks were quacking, and chickens crowed and squawked at all hours. In retrospect, I understand why the neighbor called the police. In Highland, our houses were right on top of each other, and the roosters and chickens kept crowing and squawking.

The officer looked around the place and asked questions about me.

This was the late '60s. We were fifteen minutes from downtown Chicago, and the hippie generation was in full cultural revolt. I was never involved, still have never done one drug in my life. I was just a geeky kid with a backyard zoo.

After his tour, the police officer said to my mom, "Hey, if this is what a kid has to do to stay out of trouble, you tell him to get more chickens, more ducks, and more pigeons."

I couldn't believe it when she told me. I had official backing right away.

Not long after I started going with George to the livestock sales and bird shows, my little zoo acquired its first exotic.

Maybe trading our beagle for a monkey wasn't the right thing to do. But at the time, the deal made sense to me and the trader.

George invited me to a livestock sale in St. John, Indiana, and I brought Ralph the beagle along for the trip. George went about his business, and I was walking around when I saw a man with a For Sale sign. Inside a birdcage, a squirrel monkey peered out. I stopped short, amazed by the tiny monkey that would fit in the palm of my hand.

The man said the monkey cost fifteen dollars. That was like fifteen hundred to me. I just didn't have the money. But I noticed how much the man liked Ralph.

I said, "How about trading? The monkey for the dog."

It was a deal. I couldn't believe it.

Back home, I snuck the monkey into my bedroom. I was in heaven. Oh, my gosh, I had a monkey! He came with the name Charlie.

When Mom saw him, she said, "What's this?"

I explained that I'd been with George at the sale and traded the beagle for the monkey. My mom rarely scolded me unless I did something really wrong, and this time I feared I'd gone too far. But surprisingly, she was okay with it. Mom had four kids and the grocery and garden center businesses, so perhaps a monkey in the house seemed the least of her worries.

The monkey was really popular with the neighbor kids. They loved to give him seeds and grapes and watch him climb up my shoulder. With that monkey, my little backyard zoo grew once again.

But then my father was diagnosed with cancer. Life was about to change abruptly.

BUD DeYOUNG

CHAPTER THREE
Stepping Forward

Teddy Bear had lived most of his life at Henes Park. He was a four-hundred-pound black bear who spent his days pacing a sixteen-by-sixteen enclosure with a cement floor. Visitors to the city park complained about the small space, and the outcry opened the doors for me to bring him to the zoo.

When Teddy Bear arrived, he was twenty-eight. A bear's life span generally tops out around thirty, so Teddy Bear was an old fella. For the first month, I quarantined him from the other bears in a similar enclosure to the one he'd always known.

Then the day came when I moved him out into the large bear habitat. We watched in anticipation to see what he'd do.

When Teddy Bear felt the earth under him, he sat down, lifted his paws, and stared at the green grass between his toes. He didn't know what it was. The image brings tears to my eyes every time I remember it.

Then he began to pace again. For weeks, Teddy Bear walked sixteen feet back and forth. He simply couldn't fathom that he had room to explore. The other bears terrified him; he'd never seen another bear.

Sometimes I wonder what made Teddy Bear take that first step outside this sixteen-foot invisible boundary, but at last, he did. Eventually, he integrated with the other bears as if he'd been with them his entire life.

A year later, at the age of twenty-nine, Teddy Bear passed away. Though it wasn't unexpected, I felt a true loss and wished that old bear could have had another dozen years with grass beneath his feet. But at least his final year was spent among other bears and with space to roam.

Teddy Bear enjoyed his new large home full of trees, grass, and friends to swim with in the pond.

BUD DeYOUNG

We live by the seasons. Not only us at the DeYoung Family Zoo but most folks in the Upper Peninsula and, I suppose, all across farms and ranches the country over.

But when you have exotic animals that are not equipped for the cold or able to handle the heat, there's work involved to not just keep them alive but thriving in this environment of climate extremes. The winters often drop below zero degrees Fahrenheit, and the stifling summers top out at a humid one hundred degrees.

During the summer, the zoo is open to the public seven days a week. The gates unlock at ten in the morning, but we've already been up before the sun doing chores, running errands, caring for the animals, and preparing for our visitors. The rest of the day is filled with interactions with our visitors who come from all over the country and the world. Ever since our zoo was on Nat Geo WILD for a season, we've drawn in people from as far away as Japan and Germany.

Every half hour after opening, we have Animal Encounters under the big tent. Our summer volunteers help out in various functions, including giving visitors the chance to interact with baby animals, exotics, reptiles, and, of course, Louie the chimp. I always take this opportunity to educate the public about the individual animals and to discuss conservation.

Between one and two in the afternoon, it's Big Cat Feeding. Carrie and I are together during this time, showing visitors the various habitats of big cats. Education is our main priority, and we also toss in giant slabs of meat to the tigers, African lions, mountain lions, hyenas, and panthers. All our animals have names, and we introduce visitors to as many of them as possible. People often write about how much they love watching the Big Cat Feeding.

We move from there to the Reptile Show at the alligator pond. We want visitors to have a memorable experience with creatures from the wild kingdom, and the crowd can't help but be awed by Carrie diving in with the gators. She'll come up to one and talk about its teeth, the strength of its jaw, and its thick armored exterior.

Returning to the big tent, we complete the day by bringing out some reptiles for the final Animal Encounter.

At four in the afternoon, the gates close and it's back to chores, feedings, cleaning habitats, and picking up produce and food donated by local grocery and feed stores. Also in the mornings or evenings, I drive to various ranches to collect beef and then set to work cutting it up.

Sometimes we have overnight guests camping on the property, or we decide to treat the volunteers. Then it's barbecue night by the tiger ponds. Those are good times around the campfire, eating sweet corn and steaks grilled over the open fire pit. The stars blaze overhead, and I remember how amazed I was when I first saw them in the

BUD DeYOUNG

Upper Peninsula, so bright compared to the dull night sky in Highland, Indiana.

The summer months fly by faster than I expect. After Labor Day, we leap into autumn mode when we become intent on winter preparations. We move the exotic animals indoors or into warm habitats, which sometimes include our own house.

The reptiles go inside first. The alligators and monitor lizards came in this year right after Labor Day. Next are the tropical birds, warthogs, kangaroos, wallabies, binturongs, ring-tailed lemurs, bonnet macaques, Patagonian cavies, African crested porcupines, and baboons.

During September and October, we're open Wednesday through Sunday. Then around November 1, we're closed to the public except by appointment.

Winter is the harsh time; it's about survival.

The income we make in the summer months feeds us in the winter. When the snows sweep across the forests and ranch lands, we work in the frigid temperatures to feed and care for the outdoor animals and protect the indoor ones.

Take Wallace the hippo, for example. He needs an eighty-five-degree habitat at all times. How is that possible in the freezing Upper Peninsula winters? Well, it takes one enormous woodstove the size of a large shed and a whole lot of firewood.

Many of the animals remain outside: the wolves, lions,

tigers, foxes, badgers, and leopards. The black bears and grizzlies head to their dens for hibernation. The animals from the North American region or the upper latitudes around the world are prepared for winter. They fatten up and grow thick coats and fur. The farm animals have barns and yards to go in and out of as they wish. However, they all need food. When the grass is buried beneath the snow, feeding four hundred animals is a daunting task.

Most of my winter chores are out in the cold: chopping firewood, cleaning habitats, and cutting up the beef that local ranchers donate to me. My headstone should say, "He was a professional poop cleaner and meat cutter."

Every year I tell myself I'll build a heated indoor cutting room before I lose a finger or an entire hand while cutting meat with half my body numb from the cold. But then I choose other projects, like constructing Wallace's pool decking in his winter home, a larger house for the bears, and habitats for the skunks and the new pack of wolves. So this winter I'll be cutting in the cold again.

When spring blossoms, we all—human, animal, reptile, and plant alike—come alive. The bears yawn and stretch as they come out of hibernation, the wolves and camels get all straggly as thick fur and hides start shedding, babies are born and run kicking through the new green grass, the trees open up their leaves, and hopes of warmth and rebirth grow with each day. The animals kept inside are released, and I'm sure even the gators grin. I take one deep

BUD DeYOUNG

breath in the morning and dive into the work; after all, we've got visitors coming and our big Memorial Day opening to prepare for.

At times people ask me why. Why do I live like this? Why get stretched out every which way? Why continue insane seasons of work and more work year after year?

I don't need to consider my answer. There are thousands of stories I can tell.

And that image of Teddy Bear looking at the grass between his toes is a good one.

Back in the 1960s, I was a kid who desperately wanted to live on a farm. After many years, my parents were ready to pursue that as well.

Dad and Mom started looking at farms in St. John, Indiana. I would stay up at night drawing plans for chicken coops and pigeon cages. The move fell through in 1969 when Dad was diagnosed with colon cancer. All the focus went toward getting Dad well.

Illness changed everything. I was sixteen, my brother, Randy, was fourteen, and our sisters, Leanne and Kari, were twelve and ten. Randy and I had worked at the grocery store and garden center for years by this time, and suddenly we were needed more than ever.

Immediately my father had surgery, cutting out half his colon. He also suffered from diabetes. Between the two diseases, he was quite sick and always at the hospital. Mom drove Dad nearly five hours to a St. Louis hospital while my grandma, Aunt Ruth, Aunt June, or Aunt Annalee stayed with us kids.

But Dad progressively grew worse. His eyesight faltered from the diabetes, and though surgery was supposed to help, it never worked.

Finally, there was a lull when Dad felt a little better. He came home and went right back to work at the grocery store. He'd become legally blind, but he painted signs anyway—the prices of bananas and apples, for example. He was a great artist. Everyone liked him, and customers were really glad to see him back.

Dad sold me his old Ford Country Squire since my parents needed a better vehicle to drive to St. Louis for Dad's treatments and surgery. I was sixteen, and even though it was a station wagon, I relished the freedom that came from four wheels instead of two.

Dad supplied the produce for three grocery stores, and he made me the principal buyer and delivery truck driver. I'd never driven a semi, but before long I was good at it, and I liked being outside and on the road. I searched for the best prices and quality of produce just like Dad had taught me. I went to the Watermark and Benton Harbor to pick out Michigan peaches, apples of every kind, bing cherries, and whatever was in season.

Around this time, George Dragic invited Randy and me to Michigan's Upper Peninsula for the first time. We took George's old Ford Econoline. It looked half van, half pickup with the tailgate and open bed. The back was loaded with wire and birdcages containing various species of poultry and quail for George's customers. We drove north through the towns and cities of Illinois, delivering and picking up supplies and animals, then watched the vast green farmlands of Wisconsin inch by as we traveled forty-five miles an hour, tops. That four-hundred-mile drive took two long days, and I'm sure Randy and I drove George crazy with our asking, "Are we there yet?"

At last, we crossed the border into the Upper Peninsula of Michigan where the forests grew dense and encroached on the farms and ranches that had carved out pastures for horses and cattle. The air was sweet and the sky a vivid blue. At night, the stars crowded on top of each other with a brilliance I'd rarely seen in my entire life.

One of George's customers was Dave Truitt. Everyone called him Dutch. The Truitt farm had all kinds of geese, chickens, turkeys, and other farm animals. Dutch and his wife, Juanita, had four children: Betsy, Chuck, Jeanie, and Penny. Every member of the Truitt family was an animal nut, but these kids weren't like the kids I knew in the city. They were logging and farming tough. My brother and I had some catching up to do, but we were all fast friends.

In my heart, I wanted to be a farm kid just like them. The sky was vast, the woods wild and filled with animals. It felt like home.

George Dragic had opened a life-changing door by introducing me to Penny Truitt and to the land that would become home.

CHAPTER FOUR
Chimp Rescues

Our chimpanzee Louie bottle-feeds a baby hyena. He holds the baby gently, cuddling and kissing its head.

Louie loves the other animals at the zoo. He's best with the newborns or very young critters. He has bottle-fed tiger cubs, hyenas, and piglets. He views the older animals as playmates and runs around the yard, wrestling with the dogs.

His favorite friend is his dingo, Janis. Janis and Louie have grown up together and are bonded like siblings. They hang out every day, eating and sleeping next to each other. Now that Louie is growing older, the little fella chooses to spend more time with Janis than with Carrie and me.

Louie will live in his room with his attached chimp yard for another six months to a year. We are seeing the signs that it's time to move him into the primate facility, and I must admit it's a little heartbreaking.

But until then, Louie enjoys being part of the zoo and interacting with both people and animals of every type. Visitors are always amazed to see how loving he can be.

Chimpanzees have gotten bad press in recent years. It's not the fault of the chimp. People try making them into pets or treat them like a human child, but chimpanzees are not designed for domestication.

The mistake is understandable, I suppose. Louie is shockingly humanlike. Primates share 98 percent of the same DNA as humans. In the wild, they are social animals, living in family units and communities. They adapt to various habitats from rain forest to forest to grassland. Chimpanzees even make and use tools to perform functions, such as cracking open seeds and nuts with stones, digging insects from logs or nests with sticks, and soaking up water with leaves. Though they most often walk on all fours—or "knuckle walk"—chimps can walk and stand upright. In captivity, they've been taught basic sign language. They are similar to us in many ways.

Louie came into our lives through a long series of events that spanned over six years. It began when Carrie and I were having a rare night of watching television. The program was about a chimp rescue in Florida that saved the primates from medical research labs, abusive environments, and other unhealthy situations. While this rescue was doing great work, the program said that this and other facilities were full.

During the commercial, Carrie and I looked at each other, and without discussion we both knew that somehow this would become our future.

Soon afterward, there seemed to be a string of stories about chimps in captivity attacking people. The media made it appear as if chimpanzees were dangerous instead of clarifying that almost always it's the human at fault in these situations.

Carrie and I worked on a plan. If we created a chimp rescue, we could save animals and also educate people, bringing back the wonder of these incredible and extremely intelligent creatures.

As we researched the idea and talked to experts, we were encouraged to familiarize ourselves with chimpanzees by adopting a baby chimp first. This would give us real knowledge of the primates in a healthy environment before we took on chimps that had been in bad situations. Rescued chimps often have a lot of emotional, physical, and mental issues.

Carrie and I weighed this decision long and hard. We knew it would not only be expensive but a lifelong commitment since chimps live to be around seventy-eight. During the chimpanzee's first four to five years, our lives would completely revolve around one animal, though we had several hundred others to care for as well. Those years would mean constant interaction, just as raising a human child would. Then, after these formative years, the

IT'S A WILD LIFE

chimpanzee would need to be with other chimps.

While we progressed down this path, we decided on one major condition. We didn't want to obtain just any chimp. We wanted an orphaned chimp, one that needed us. It took six years for Louie to come into our lives.

Louie's mom was a chimpanzee that had retired from an entertainment venue and was living at an out-of-state zoo. She'd been trained as a performer and didn't know how to be a mother.

On March 21, 2010, she gave birth to Louie on a snowy night, then placed him on the cold ground near the front gate to the chimp habitat. A zookeeper heard her screaming and crying and went out to investigate. He found tiny newborn Louie in the snow with placenta still attached and the mother going crazy in the trees overhead.

Louie could have easily died in that weather, but he was a fighter right from the beginning.

We got a call from the zoo. When Carrie and I heard Louie's story, we both wanted to cry. This chimp needed us. He'd been abandoned by his mother, and we knew this was our chimp.

We had a few challenges, however. First, it was the end of winter, the time of year when our finances are most depleted. We knew that since chimps are very desired, the zoo couldn't give us much time. It seemed impossible to bring Louie home, even with our immediate yes.

Carrie went to the zoo to meet Louie and to be trained

to care for him. When she returned, she brought videos, photographs, and stories that only further struck our hearts. I stared at the pictures of that little chimp, who was the size of a soda can and weighed only three pounds four ounces.

We had to make our final decision. Again, we discussed the lifelong commitment. We also knew that Louie would wrap around our hearts as a human child would but that we'd have to let him go as he matured. This meant getting other siblings and building a family for him as well as continuing our commitment to create a chimp rescue.

Though we tried to weigh the decision carefully, we knew bringing home this chimpanzee was what we were supposed to do.

With several zoo projects already slated for the summer, I headed in to see my banker for a loan.

Right before Carrie was ready to return to Louie's home zoo, our lemur birthed twins. Those babies fit into the palms of our hands. But their mother abandoned them, and no amount of coaxing could get her to take care of them. Carrie brought the babies inside the house and began the round-the-clock job of keeping them warm and feeding them by syringe.

We decided I'd go spend time with Louie, and I brought along our good friend Bobby Francis. When I first saw Louie, he looked so fragile; it was like handling a basket of eggs.

The facility taught us a lot in the days we were there. They also had me spend time with the adult chimpanzees but warned me about the male that didn't like people. He had a habit of sneaking over to the water and coming near the fence line as if he weren't paying attention to the person on the other side. Then unexpectedly, he'd spray a mouthful of water all over the person.

When I saw the male, I ignored him and sat near the fence and acted like I was eating ants off a stick. When the male came close, I put the stick through the fence so the male chimp could eat the ants. It wasn't long before he had his back turned toward me, wanting me to scratch it. The zookeepers were pretty amazed, but I joked about being half chimp myself.

Soon it was time to bring Louie home.

But first we had to ask our friends and neighbors to give us some time to settle in. Our community is incredibly supportive of us, and they get excited when we bring in new animals. This time was unique. Louie's immune system was weak after being abandoned in the cold without getting the nutritional benefits of his mother's milk. We kept him quarantined for a while, fearing he'd get sick or over-whelmed with visitors. It was much like having a newborn child: Carrie and I alternately cared for him around the clock. It wasn't long until Louie grew healthy and strong.

A chimp's rate of growth is similar to a child's. Despite the numerous developmental and genetic comparisons,

BUD DeYOUNG

we always have in mind that he's not a human. He's a chimpanzee.

Louie became part of every single thing we do, day and night, rain or shine, at the zoo or away. We love all our animals spread across the zoo—from the goats, pigs, and cows to the foxes, bears, and hyenas. Big or small, rodent or reptile, no animal is considered less than another in our eyes. We nurture and give our lives for all of them. But for a long time Carrie and I didn't do anything together without one of us constantly at the house with Louie. We still rarely do. But we don't mind; this is what we waited six years to experience. We couldn't have guessed how deeply a chimp could become woven into our hearts.

As Louie outgrew our initial concerns for him, we were able to train half a dozen nannies—including Elouise Goffin, Kathy Youngworth, Bobby Francis, and Cindy Zeratsky—for when we absolutely had to go to a fundraiser or other event. Most were moms who had experience with both animals and children.

During his first year, Louie had a few colds and ear infections. With all the concern of new parents, we took him to our vet and also a local pediatrician. The pediatrician prescribed amoxicillin, the same antibiotic used to cure a child. We hovered over Louie that first year, and we constantly called the out-of-state zoo to ask questions. That's one thing I learned long ago: don't be afraid to ask questions.

As the months passed, Carrie and I cheered as Louie started crawling and then finally walked, first knuckle walking, then upright for periods of time. As he got around more, I built Louie his own room with a connected outdoor habitat. In 2011, Louie finally got to play in his yard. He ran around, swinging on the ropes and playing with his toys as a child would on his first trip to a playground.

At the writing of this book, Louie is over two years of age and requires less personal care but more attention. He needs constant mental stimulation through social interaction and play. About sixteen hours a day, he's on my shoulders or Carrie's or, in the summer months, a staff member's. He enjoys riding around the zoo with me on the four-wheeler during feeding time.

Louie also enjoys the zoo visitors. We bring him to the tent for Animal Encounters, and he charms the guests with his antics. Often I give someone the chance to feed him his bottle, which he slurps up in less than a minute. Louie especially likes the ladies, senior citizens, and people with special needs. Somehow he senses that they need more care.

However, Louie does not play well with children. He's just too strong and doesn't know how to be gentle with them. We always instruct the kids to stay at a distance where they can watch Louie but not touch him.

Louie views unfamiliar teen and adult males as rivals and can become a little aggressive with them. He beats his

BUD DeYOUNG

chest as if giving out a challenge, then jumps and climbs up their arms and heads. It's all playful, but his strength can be intimidating.

Already at age two, he has lifted more than two hundred pounds. When full grown, Louie will be approximately two hundred fifty pounds and fifty inches tall. His intelligence will be equivalent to a five-year-old child's, and he'll have the strength of five men. Though his jaw structure is different from ours, Louie's organs are the same.

The bond that Carrie and I have forged with Louie has only enhanced our desire to create a primate rescue facility. Around the country there are chimpanzees that need homes. Other chimps are acquired as babies, but then their owners discover they can't be controlled and seek out new homes for them. The public perception that chimps are dangerous frustrates us to no end, because chimps are not meant to live like humans. Then there are chimps used for medical research and euthanized. The thought of it is just deplorable, especially when I look into Louie's eyes. All of this remains with us and drives us toward providing a haven for chimps in need.

In coming years we will bring in a sibling for Louie, and after that, he'll move from the house into his own habitat. We plan to relocate the wolf habitat to the section designated for North American animals. Then Carrie's dad will build a new primate habitat in its place. Our plans are for a very large area to accommodate Louie and his future family members.

I've instructed a guy to work on a Primadome this winter that will be used as a shelter. But at this time, we've missed several chances to adopt chimps. We recently passed on a brother for Louie. Our funds have kept us from moving forward. I have to find a balance for my dreams, I suppose.

Since childhood, I have not been a good manager of my dreams. When I get an idea in my head, I work my ass off to make it come true. Maybe one day it'll all catch up to me. But as I see Louie and his dingo Janis play chase across the yard, I can't help but think the best way to turn a dream into reality is to give it all you've got.

CHAPTER FIVE
Passion in Pain

Blazing through the pine forests of Michigan's Upper Peninsula, the deciduous trees are like flames of gold, orange, and red. The wolves move regally in their thick winter coats; the bears have fattened up and will soon head into their dens to hibernate; the squirrels pack away nuts into stumps and logs. All over the zoo, preparations are being made for winter.

The gates are closed on Mondays and Tuesdays now. Today, instead of the voices of visitors, the crisp air is cut with the sounds of saws, hammers, and concrete trucks churning loads of wet cement. We're taking a break from moving the exotic critters indoors to put in permanent flooring in our hippo's winter pool house.

Carrie's father, Bart Gagnon, came up from Pulaski, Wisconsin, to work on Wallace's eighty-by-forty-foot heated indoor pool building. He's also tackling other projects in the race to beat the cold. With my extensive ideas for the zoo, Bart is an enormous asset when he volunteers his many skills. He deserves a plaque for all the help he's provided over the years.

My plans for Wallace's winter and summer habitats are slowly coming along in stages. I'd hoped to put in new piping throughout the indoor pool that would automatically keep Wallace's water fresh to avoid the chore of cleaning it out every other week. Another big project pending is a walled connector between Wallace's summer and winter homes. It would make it easier to move Wallace between the two habitats. Last year Bart and I partially completed it, and I'm impatient to be done with it by this winter. But it's not going to happen.

Yet I'm grateful for all these men, helping to mark off another important task on my ever-growing list. Since we first brought the baby hippo home, his winter swimming pool has had a liner on the bottom. It isn't working well, especially as Wallace has grown and could easily rip through the liner with his feet.

Matt and Dave Kubiak from Pool Works in Green Bay, Wisconsin, are pressure spraying a new floor of concrete pool decking. The brothers are experts in spas and pools. Usually such a project would cost around twenty thousand dollars. They charged me only six hundred dollars to cover the cost of gas to drive their rig up here.

The generous donations toward the project don't stop there. Peters Concrete out of Gillette, Wisconsin, delivered two truckloads of cement mix in the churning drums, yet they gave me a bill for only one.

All day, we put our sweat and energy into Wallace's house. By the end, the new pool decking is complete and Bart has redone the lighting, giving the hippo house a much more professional look. I stand back with arms crossed, admiring the work.

After it's dry, I fill up the pool and prepare to move Wallace in. He is not cooperative, despite how much I tell him he'll enjoy the improvements. While Wallace obeys many of my commands, he doesn't work with me when I need him to get into the trailer. For days, I try different tactics to lure him inside. It takes a week.

All my plans for expansion, new animal habitats, and more efficient facilities remind me that I've continued building on the same dream I had as a kid. I'll sketch ideas onto scraps of paper or stay up late working on my schemes just as I did back in Highland. There was only one time in my life when my plans came to a sudden stop. For a time, I wondered if they died along with the people I loved.

I was never popular in high school. I was never involved in sports; I wasn't very athletic. My grades were far down the list of priorities. I hung out in the biology lab taking care of the boa constrictor and iguanas. After school I went to my dad's grocery stores and worked till it was time to put the produce in the coolers at closing. Girls weren't interested in the odd animal guy who worked all the time, so I never had a girlfriend or even a date. I just didn't have a big social life.

In the fall of 1970 when I was seventeen, George Dragic took me to upper Michigan. We hauled different kinds of livestock to the farmers as well as various birds, including waterfowl and chickens. Over the previous summer, my brother and I were invited to stay a week by North Lake, where George's brother lived. We helped with the dairy cows and also spent time at the Truitt farm.

At Dutch Truitt's ranch by Hayward Lake, I went deer hunting for the first time. I'd never gone hunting before, and surprisingly, it didn't conflict with my love for animals. I understood it. Everybody in that area hunted and raised animals for food. It was how to get meat—and still is today—for the winter. The more I came to know the locals and their way of life, the more I loved it.

Penny Truitt and I were a year apart, and at first, she was just another girl about my age. Penny and her friends took me to a camp party. To these tough logging girls, I must have been just this skinny kid from Indiana. As I mentioned, I didn't hang out with girls much. It was a different world to me. But at that time, Penny and I were only friends.

My life was still back in Indiana, and I always looked

forward to resuming that busy life of helping my dad. As the holidays approached, our family couldn't have guessed it would be our last Christmas with our father. It would be months before we knew that.

Then in May of 1971, I graduated high school and practically ran out of the place. With their medical expenses, my parents didn't have money for college, and I didn't care about college anyway. I wanted to get to the woods and country. But as my father's health continued to decline, I was needed to drive the semi and supply the grocery stores with produce.

In July, the call came that Dad wasn't doing very well. My brother, sisters, and I knew our father was very sick, but he seemed invincible in our eyes. We couldn't imagine death getting the best of him.

My grandparents drove my siblings and me to St. Margaret in Hammond, Indiana, right away. When I saw my father in that hospital bed, I was stunned. He was bad.

The doctor asked us to follow him into the hall, where he told us that Dad had only a short time to live.

The day was July 13, 1971. It was my eighteenth birthday and the day I watched my dad take his last breath.

Even all these years later, the memories of that day and of my father's funeral are hard to think about. All my hopes and plans came to a crashing halt. My mother was devastated, and as the oldest son, I felt the weight of worry and responsibility for her and my three younger siblings.

But mostly, I couldn't grasp the fact that my father was gone.

There have been many times when life loomed large and daunting. It's part of the journey, I guess, but this was a tough time for all of us. Of course, we moved on, but at that time, I couldn't quite see how.

My father is still close to me. Sometimes I wonder what he'd think of this land and what I've built. I know he'd love to be here, working on the hippo habitat and being part of the zoo. He taught me how to work hard and give everything my best, so his spirit lives on. And that spirit is what raised me up after his death to move forward, to keep sketching ideas and dreaming big.

CHAPTER SIX
Good-byes and New Beginnings

I was finally an adult. Instead of celebrating, I stared at the funeral program with my birthday printed as the date of my father's death. Dad and I also shared a name, with me being the junior. Even to this day, it's strange to know that my name and eighteenth birthday are chiseled into my father's headstone.

I had never been to a funeral until my father's. My family was in a state of shock when we arrived at the funeral home for viewing and then for the service itself. Family arrived from everywhere: my four aunts, my mom's parents, Dad's mother, and his five sisters and four brothers.

There were also five hundred people who came from all over the area to honor my father. The funeral home didn't have enough seats for those who showed up to pay their last respects.

Dad knew so many people from the community, the

garden center, and the grocery stores, and he made friends and would talk to everyone. I can't imagine anyone who didn't like my dad. His death at such a young age of forty-four years took everyone by surprise. They'd known he was sick, even that he'd gone blind, but suddenly, Harold Lloyd DeYoung Sr. was gone from this earth, and they were there to show their admiration for him.

Memories of Dad's ventures, like the years we sold Christmas trees for extra money, returned. We hauled beautiful noble pines, balsam firs, and Scotch pines down from lower Michigan to sell for five and seven dollars each. Once, the semi was loaded so high we ended up with most of a town's Christmas lights dragging behind us.

Through the fog of grief, what is still vivid in my mind is my mother's anguish. My strong and vivacious mother was broken by the loss, and I felt utterly helpless, unable to take away her pain or offer any real comfort to her.

In the months after the funeral, Mom was in rough shape. She and Dad had been so close. They'd been very much in love, and their lives were woven together in everything. While Mom raised us, she had also worked at the stores at Dad's side. When he was sick, they were never apart. Mom took him to his treatments in St. Louis and stayed at the hospital with him. She was Dad's right and left hands, quite literally, when he went blind.

With my father gone, there was no possibility of leaving. While Mom is one of the strongest people I've ever known, she had three children still at home. As the new man of the house, I didn't just feel obligated to help take care of them; I wanted to.

When I told my mother I was staying home and would continue to work in Dad's business, she became upset. "I want you to follow through with your plans," she told me. "We'll be all right." It was the last response I had expected.

My mom was always supportive of my wild schemes and everything I wanted to do. In fact, people couldn't believe the things she allowed—animals living in our house, my digging up the backyard to build ponds and stealing screens from our windows to make pens for animals.

And there were plenty more examples. Once, Mom was surprised by possums in the garage when she took out the garbage. Similarly, during the time of my father's illness when my grandparents were staying with us, Grandma had a surprise. She was up late ironing clothes when a little troop of button quail emerged from beneath my bedroom door. I'd had them in an incubator in my room, and they hatched in the night. They were so small that they fit right under the door.

Mom didn't love having the animals in the house, and sometimes she'd get on me about the mess or keeping certain critters inside. But even today, she still believes a child should be allowed to do what he or she loves. "Anyone who can follow their dream . . . well, isn't that what everyone dreams of doing—getting to live what they love?" she says.

When I asked Mom what her dream was, she laughed and said she didn't know. Sometimes I wonder if her dream was to help her kids dream and follow what they were meant to do.

However, at that time in our lives, Mom needed me. She was worried about paying the $79 monthly mortgage bill. That's an amazing number to consider today, but this was when gas was about 12 cents a gallon.

I knew enough from my father, my upbringing, and our extended family, who stepped up to care for us during Dad's illness, that deserting my mom and siblings was out of the question.

She could be upset with me, but I wasn't leaving.

The next year wasn't easy, but we weren't alone.

My mom had three sisters: June, Annalee, and Ruth. Aunt Annalee and Aunt June never married or had children, so my brother, my sisters, and I were the focus of their attention. They loved to spoil us. During the time of my father's treatment, our aunts and grandparents took care of us. We had never lacked attention when my father was sick and our mother was gone with him.

My aunties did so much for me as a kid growing up. Like Mom, they encouraged my interest in animals, and it seemed I could do no wrong in their eyes.

We were also the only grandchildren of my mother's parents, and they doted on us.

Though we were grieving the loss of Dad, we were surrounded with love from all sides.

I kept driving the semi and choosing the best produce for the grocery stores, just as Dad had taught me. We got on okay, but we missed Dad something fierce. The emptiness could be felt everywhere: in the house, at work, at the dinner table. Mom put on a strong exterior, but we knew she often cried in her room at night.

My animals kept me busy in the hours I wasn't at work. I kept bringing home new ones, birds from the swaps or various strays that I found.

Once at a family dinner with my aunts and grandparents, Mom looked up from the table and jumped in surprise. Coming down the hallway was my giant iguana. He'd learned how to open his cage and apparently thought he should be invited to dinner as well. My mom, aunts, and grandma didn't take too kindly to the green monster heading toward us.

After I caught him and returned him to my room, the family had a good laugh. So my animals served another purpose during this time of mourning.

In the autumn of 1971, I was able to go with George Dragic to upper Michigan to help at his brother's farm and hunt deer.

I saw the Truitt family, including Penny. She was a

friend to me, just as her siblings were, but that was about it.

With all my work hours, in addition to helping out the family, I saved money. When I was ready for a new car, I sold the station wagon and took my savings to the Greater Chicago Auto Auction with my uncle Glen. I bought a 1971 Corvette Stingray.

It's amazing what a car can do. Not just the speed, the handling, and the way it made me feel behind the wheel with all that power beneath the gas pedal. That Corvette also changed my social life.

Overnight, I went from having no girlfriend to having girls all over the place. Suddenly I was popular. I was the guy with a good job and a Corvette Stingray. It was an interesting experience but not one I had time to fully take advantage of. I dated a few girls, but my life was full with work and my animals.

1979: George and I snowmobiling.

The Vietnam War was in full swing during these years. It was covered in the papers and on the news. There were protests in Chicago, and worn-out vets returned to little fanfare compared with returning soldiers of the past.

The war and its effects barely touched my life for a long time. My name, like every other eligible male's, was put into the draft lottery. We were numbered by our birth-dates. I think my number was in the three hundred fifties out of three hundred sixty-five for the year. The numbers were put into a rolling drum, and those picked were drafted into the military. I wasn't chosen.

After about a year, the other owners of Dad's grocery stores decided to buy Mom out. I guess they didn't like having a woman as a partner. That was another blow for Mom, but she is a tough person, and I know she's the one who made me as strong as I am. The loss of the business she'd built with my dad was another challenge she would overcome.

I still drove the semi for the new owners, saved money, and helped at home.

By 1973, Mom was working at a new job. She became the head secretary for the CEO at Prudential in Chicago.

That year, my brother turned eighteen and immediately enlisted in the Army. Randy made a good case for why he'd signed up, and I began to seriously consider enlisting as well. Mom had only the girls at home, and they were in high school, and she continued to urge us to follow the path that called to us.

Eventually, I went down and talked to the recruiter. He had a lot to say. I was intrigued and ready to move forward with the next stage of my life, and the Army was looking like a great choice. But as we talked, I wasn't quite ready to enlist. I had something I needed to do first.

"I'm going on a fishing trip. As soon as I'm back, I want to talk more," I told the recruiter.

My fishing trip was in June of 1973. I was twenty and headed up to the Upper Peninsula on my own.

Of course, my Corvette made me stand out there even more than usual. I was still a city boy to everyone, no matter how many times I'd come up with George, worked at his brother's dairy or the Truitts' farm, or gone deer hunting or fishing with them.

One time I took Dutch Truitt out in the Corvette. "Hey, Dutch, I can take this from zero to ninety in about a hundred yards," I said.

The look on his face said, *Wow, this is one crazy kid from Indiana.*

After all those years, I'd become pretty close to the Truitt family.

Penny had a one-year-old daughter now. She was a cute little thing, that Carry Lynn. The father wasn't in the picture, and Penny and I started spending more time together.

Now I stood at the intersection of two potential paths that could forever alter my future. One was to join the military and leave the Midwest. The other tugged at my love of the woods and the lifestyle I'd come to admire in the people of upper Michigan. That path also included Penny Truitt.

When she said, "Why don't we get married?" the choice wasn't hard to make.

Carrie with one of the hyenas. Don't try this at home, kids! These guys love her like she's one of their own, but Carrie has the utmost respect for these critters. Her goal is to educate and inspire people to love all animals.

CHAPTER SEVEN
Moving North

We've been frantically moving animals indoors for the winter. The weather forecast is predicting an October snowstorm, a month earlier than usual. We are not ready. With exotic animals and reptiles that can't sustain the frigid temperatures, we have no choice but to get prepared no matter what it takes. And so, our house is filled with animals.

A few weeks ago, three baby hyenas were born. They were born early, at night, and the mom was restless.

With the weather turning and the babies weak, we made the hard decision to remove them from their habitat and their mother. This is never easy. We feel terrible when it happens, but sometimes it's necessary for the babies' survival. It is hard on the mom and on us, especially Carrie. She loves her hyenas.

I had to tranquilize the mother hyena and gate up the male to get the babies. The female would give her life to keep her babies from being moved, but if they remain, the cold will kill them. Carrie has already switched them to a bottle for the coming months. In springtime, they'll be returned to their mother.

The count for critters inside the house goes like this: three baby hyenas, four prairie dogs, an albino skunk, six New Guinea singing pups, four Chihuahuas, Maggie May, our bonnet macaque, and of course Louie and the regular three dogs. I told Carrie that I didn't want another pig in the house, but one morning recently, I walked into the bathroom and there was a Meishan pig in the tub. Carrie never listens to me; she does just what she wants.

Our enclosed porch is now temporary housing for two warthogs, a beaver, and two kangaroos. Wallace is safely in his indoor hippo habitat, and we brought the alligators and other reptiles into the building with the tropical birds and other exotics.

My plan for winter preparations has been tossed out with a storm disrupting my process. The weather doesn't much abide by my schedule. Sometimes it seems our lives are shoved this way and that by outside forces that lead us down a path we can only see clearly in retrospect.

In 1974, my brother left for the Army while my mother and two sisters remained in Indiana. I was getting married, but I fought with guilt over leaving Mom. She kept pushing me to live my own life. "That's what a man does," she told

BUD DeYOUNG

me. "Your father would be proud."

As I worked my last days driving the truck, the other tough decision was made. My little backyard zoo couldn't go with me.

My squirrel monkey had passed away before my father's death. I'd had Charlie for only a year and a half, but when I'd traded our beagle for him, he was already advanced in age.

I went to a bird swap and auction and said good-bye to my pigeons, chickens, ducks, and geese.

After all those years of having birds and animals around the place, the house and yard felt empty. The neighbors were probably cheering my departure after putting up with early-morning rooster crows and pigeon droppings on their yards, roofs, and porch eaves.

Before I moved out, I sold my car. By then I had a '73, which I'd traded the first one to get. When my future father-in-law said, "You won't have much need for that up here," I knew he was right. I bought a '69 Ford pickup, something much more practical for life in the woods.

With everything wrapped up, it was finally time for me to move north.

Penny Truitt and I married in 1974 at the Gethsemane Lutheran Church in Wallace, Michigan. Our families attended, including Mom, my sisters, my aunts, and my grandparents. My brother was granted leave from the Army and, wearing his military uniform, served as my best man. Our reception in the town hall beneath the firehouse was home catered, and we danced to a polka band, as was popular in that time and area.

When I moved to upper Michigan, it wasn't like relocating; it was more like coming into my own. I had found my place in the world.

As soon as we married, I adopted Penny's daughter, Carry Lynn, and gave her the DeYoung last name. For me, it was great having a kid right from the start. I had always liked kids, and though I didn't know much about raising a child, my father had been a good example and I caught on pretty quickly. Life was changing rapidly as I became an instant husband and father in a completely different environment.

I worked with my father-in-law peeling and hauling poplar. For just five thousand dollars, Dutch and Juanita, Penny's parents, sold us an old 1964 Detroit mobile home and the forty acres that the DeYoung Family Zoo still resides on. Our land was so wooded that I could hardly see the road only one hundred fifty yards away from the trailer. Right off, we did some clearing. I used a late 1800s tractor I purchased to cut through the trees and brush for a garden area, yard, and driveway. I hooked up a woodstove for the coming winter. Today, some forty-seven years later, I'm still heating with wood.

I'd never fully experienced an Upper Peninsula winter, and in that little trailer, I discovered what it meant to be cold. We'd wake up in the morning and find the water in the toilet bowl had frozen in the night. The trailer was so small that I could lay in the bedroom with my head touching one wall and my feet reaching the other, and if I put my arms out I could touch the sides. But we made do. We were happy.

We had what we needed to be a family.

Bradley David DeYoung was born on April 12, 1975, less than a year after Penny and I married. I have to say, it was the best thing since sliced bread. I had my own son.

Then, jeepers, it was under two years later that we had Rebecca "Becky" Jean.

In less than three years of marriage, we had three little kids running around in that tiny trailer.

In early winter 1975, I was hired at Peck Packing in Birch Creek, Michigan. The plant processed about four hundred cattle a day. I was out on the loading dock, where I carried the quarters of beef into the waiting trucks. At first, I didn't think I'd make it. It was such backbreaking work, and the schedule was twelve to sixteen hours a day, six days a week. But before long, my muscles got used to it, and I could carry from one hundred to four hundred pounds onto a semitrailer.

It was a good thing my muscles grew stronger; I needed them to work for my father-in-law during my off hours.

For the first seven years of marriage, I was regularly

working twenty hours a day and sleeping four hours a night. I had no problem falling asleep. I'd go to bed about nine or ten o'clock and get up around two in the morning to go to the packinghouse.

Penny was left to do everything at the house and raise the children. But this was normal life for her. Her parents had raised her in the same manner.

I made three dollars an hour at the packing plant, which even in the late seventies was below minimum wage. But since I worked eighty hours a week and had my other side jobs, we were able to make it.

One side job was still working in the woods for Dutch. My father-in-law was very hard on me. He was constant drive, drive, and more drive. If a man didn't work up to Dutch's standard, then that man wasn't good enough for him. He was also extremely frugal to the point that most would call him tight.

I love my father-in-law, and he helped make me the worker that I am today. So I thank Dutch for that. And he didn't expect more than he gave. Over the course of his lifetime, he'd logged over forty forties, which meant he'd cleared forty acres forty times. He was known for his logging expertise.

In the summer, we'd peel trees, and in the autumn, we'd load up the flatbed truck and haul it to Badger Paper Mill.

In the wintertime, I worked for Dutch cutting out cedar post off the M-35 after my shift at the packinghouse.

BUD DeYOUNG

The money kept us moving. My brother-in-law Dennis DeTemple and I were out there in waist-deep snow with Dutch, and in five to six hours, we could make a hundred dollars. In the late seventies and early eighties, this was a lot of money. We felt like we were rich. It made working in the frigid temperatures worth it.

Back at our place, we had seven or eight cows that needed to be milked by hand. We also had farm animals we raised mostly for food and some as pets. Since Penny had her hands full with the house and family, my mother-in-law, Juanita, often came by and did the morning chores. She was a wonderful woman, always giving and kind. I took the evening chores.

Every fall, I also did taxidermy work, which I'd taught myself to do in Indiana when I couldn't save a critter. I enjoyed bringing animals back to life in this little way.

By 1979, our family had long since outgrown that eight-by-thirty-foot trailer. The winters, when the kids were cooped up, were especially tough for Penny. With my long hours, we were finally able to purchase a prefabricated house.

To save money, Dutch dug the basement with an attachment on his logging truck. To put in the well, he brought out a willow stick. I almost laughed as my father-in-law searched around with the stick for water. But suddenly the stick dipped down, and that's where we put the point. The earth in the Upper Peninsula is woven with springs, very artisan, and with Dutch's expertise, we didn't have much trouble finding water. I pounded with a concrete mallet, and we reached water only thirteen feet down. We put in a hand pump first, then a pump for the house.

I'm still using the same well today, and it was the only source of water for the zoo for a long time. A few years ago, I finally had another well dug near the hyenas to provide enough water for Wallace the hippo and the growing zoo. Wallace requires a lot of water, and it was a prerequisite for getting him. Back in the seventies, we spent fifty dollars for a point, but now it costs twenty thousand dollars to have a well drilled.

With the basement and well complete, we ordered the house. I went to work one morning at the packinghouse and came back to find a house sitting there. Penny and the kids were thrilled to have their own rooms and an actual home to stretch out in. Even though the house was eight hundred square feet, it felt like a mansion.

The house was twenty-five thousand dollars, and the land was five thousand. The total loan was thirty thousand dollars. Our monthly payment was one hundred dollars.

With my packinghouse job, projects with my father-in-law, our farm, and the taxidermy, I was never lacking for work. I was able to make double payments on the house, though the payments weren't that big, and I worked so much that we paid off the house in eleven years.

It still amazes me how the years pass. I can look out at this land and remember the changes; sometimes I can almost see the kids running around. The layout of our property has changed considerably but always with this house sitting on a little rise in the middle.

As the kids were growing up, we had plenty of animals. Penny had been raised on a farm, and of course I had a lifelong love of critters, so our children were bound to inherit at least some of that affection. With every year, our farm grew with chickens, cows, hogs, sheep, goats, and horses as well as the domestics. Then we added raccoons, foxes, deer, and eventually a baby bear, then more bears and tigers.

We always had a lot of dogs, at least twenty-three over the years. Then almost every spring, we'd get an orphaned fawn and raise it until autumn when we'd turn it loose.

Before the girls had bicycles, they had horses. They were barely walking when I bought them ponies. As they grew older, we moved to horses.

When Carry Lynn was about eight years old, she and her cousin Tina were racing on horseback across the field. The horses spooked, and both girls fell off. Tina broke her leg and sustained injuries, but Carry was even more severely hurt when the horse trampled her in the fall.

Penny rode in the ambulance while I drove to the hospital in Green Bay.

The doctors told us that Carry had a ruptured kidney.

She had to have surgery or she'd die.

There's nothing worse than seeing your child in pain like that.

She pulled through just fine, but after that she didn't care much for horses.

Each of the kids was unique and still is.

Carry was very smart. She did well in school and always had a compassionate heart. She completed a four-year nursing program in three years, and her professors asked her to tutor other students. Her memorization skills and photographic memory amaze me.

Bradley was an outdoorsy kid. We'd go deer or duck hunting, all for food. We didn't have a lot of money, so hunting and raising our own food was essential to survival. Sometimes Brad helped with the logging, but as he grew, he became really involved with sports, especially basketball, through the school. He would occasionally hop on a horse and take off, but horses weren't his favorite hobby. Brad was also the prankster. He was the kid teasing the horses, the dogs, and his sisters.

Becky was an apple that didn't fall far from the tree. She has a love for animals comparable to mine, and she helped me with the fledgling collection I started at the house. We raised ducks, chickens, cows, and pigs. When she was just a little thing, she helped me in the barns, milking the cows and doing the chores. A dozen dogs or cats were always following her every step.

Becky loved the horses and could get thrown, bucked off, or whatever, and she'd get back on. Most of Becky's horses came from the auction for about fifty dollars because that's all we could afford. They were generally right off the pasture or right off the mare and had never been ridden. At first when the girls were young, it was my job to break them. Later Becky took over.

Until I had my children, I'd never had my own horse. During my teenage years, I'd gone through a horse phase. I'd go with my friend Larry to horse sales in Indiana like I did with George to the bird swaps. At the sales, I'd ride the horses in the ring. Eventually I bought my own saddle and kept it in the house. I remember Mom asking me, "What's that for?" She was probably fearful that a horse would stick its head out of my closet.

The horses at our place weren't just for fun. We didn't have any four-wheelers, three-wheelers, snowmobiles, or anything like that. Transportation back and forth across the woods, a mile and a half, was generally by horseback. On our second horse, Prince, I put binder twine around his neck and rode him bareback across the woods to milk the cows. For a while, I became a really good rider.

I broke a lot of horses for Becky, but a lot of horses broke me. My sacrum in my back would go out sometimes when I was bucked off or while I was training. The pain shot like fire through my back, doubling me over so I couldn't stand up. Penny would practically carry me to the truck to drive me to the chiropractor. I'd have to crawl out of the vehicle and into the chiropractor's office for him to realign my back.

But no matter what struggles we faced, we always made it work as a family, and we even had a chance to help other people. During the kids' high school years, dozens of their friends stayed at our place. They were kids who might have had problems at their own homes. A lot of them wanted to live with Penny and me. Jeepers, there were times we had five or six kids living here besides my three kids. Our door was always open, and we never turned a kid away.

Somehow it all worked out, and we had a very good family. But even with all of this to be grateful for, there was still an old longing that wouldn't release me.

CHAPTER EIGHT
Building Life and Facing Antlers

In 1981 after seven years in the Upper Peninsula and working at the slaughterhouse, I got a job at Carpenter Cook, a grocer supply warehouse in Menominee, Michigan. They needed a driver, and I already had a chauffeur's license from my time driving the semi for my dad in Indiana.

For the first two weeks, I trained with Johnny Johnson and rode with him in the truck. Then I was on my own. When they didn't need a driver, I worked in the warehouse. We filled orders by bringing out the cases of produce. I was quick at produce picking, and my numbers were equal or above those of the experienced workers in just a few weeks.

I became a good friend of Jerry Van, Ben Steward, and Phillip Stroll, the heads of Carpenter Cook. It was a great place to be employed, like working for family. They treated me very well.

At Carpenter Cook, I drove five and six nights a week.

I always drove Saturdays because it paid extra. With this job, we had benefits, including really good insurance.

I drove mainly at night because, besides having a family, I still worked with Dutch on his farm and out in the woods to make a dime whenever I could. I'd become an above-average taxidermist and did over a hundred deer heads and bears every season. I knew what animals looked like, so I could implement that in my mounting.

Problem was, I could never say no, and it got out of hand when I took in more than I could handle. I was always doing half a dozen different jobs at the same time.

The years passed quickly with the days and seasons filled with work, more work, and family life. But that little backyard zoo in Highland, Indiana, never left me.

My mom and siblings were doing well. With Mom's encouragement, each of us went different directions to pursue what we loved.

After the Army, Randy settled in the woods and became a logger in Washington State. Kari is an artist and owns a novelty shop in Indiana. During the holidays, she decorates window displays for big stores in Chicago. Leanne followed her gifts to become a schoolteacher in Louisiana. Four children with four very different paths and Mom supported each one.

Mom was enjoying her work and sometimes came up for a visit. She loved Penny, her grandchildren, and seeing the animals, though she was probably glad to leave all those critters with us when she went home.

As I was doing all my work, I collected used wire and fencing. Once I took down an old tennis court; other times, I'd get discarded chain-link fences. With these supplies, I started building pens.

The first enclosure I built was for white-tailed deer, which were the first wild animals I housed. I'd cleared about two acres toward the front of our property, where our zoo parking lot is now located.

For some time, I'd stop in to watch the deer at local deer farms. Deer are fascinating creatures. They can leap incredible heights, and they appear so delicate, yet the males can be surprisingly fierce.

Male deer grow antlers that can easily be confused with horns. Basically, antlers are an extension of the animal's skull made of bone and are a single structure. Horns are two-part structures. They include bone on the interior, which is also an extension of the skull, and they are covered by an exterior sheath of hair follicles, similar to a human's fingernails. While antlers are shed and grow back annually, horns never shed and grow throughout the life of an animal. An exception is the pronghorn sheep, which has horns that are shed every year.

Antlers grow from the skull at a point called the pedicle. When a deer is in velvet, the antler is growing and covered in a vascular skin that supplies oxygen and nutrients to the bone. Once the antler finishes growing, usually within a few months, the velvet disappears and the bone dies. People are often surprised that the large rack of a deer doesn't just continue growing to its size over years but usually falls off every year or so, each time growing even larger than before. The size and span of antlers become important in attracting females as well as in fighting off other males.

During the autumn months, the mating season—called rut—begins. A perfectly nice deer can change dramatically during the rut. I've been on the bad end of that personality switch, and it isn't enjoyable.

During the rut, bucks rub their antlers on trees and fight one another for the right to mate with the females. This coincides with the gestational period of different species of deer so that the babies are born in the spring. There's never a season when there isn't something interesting to observe in deer if someone takes the time to watch.

After I'd been collecting wire and fencing and building enclosures for some time, I decided to get my game breeder's license. It could be purchased for forty-five dollars with no regulations on pen size.

I obtained from numerous places white-tailed and white fallow deer from individuals and various deer from Henes Park in Menominee.

White-tailed deer are medium sized and native to the United States as well as throughout North and South America, though surprisingly not in some of the western

BUD DeYOUNG

states. They have reddish-brown coats, and their fawns have white spots that help camouflage them in the springtime. The deer are distinguishable by the bright white fur on the underside of their tail.

The fallow deer are originally from western Eurasia. After about three years, their antlers become more flat and spread out, somewhat like that of a moose. Often people think my white fallow deer are albino, but they're actually a variant of the breed. The fawns are cream colored while the adults become pure white, especially in the winter.

At one time, I had close to thirty-five deer on our land with a variety of bloodlines.

I traded some deer for an elk, and that was one big creature. Elk are the largest of the deer family and one of the biggest land mammals in North America and eastern Asia. This was one gorgeous fella. Male elk can be up to nine feet tall from hoof to antler tips and have antlers that sometimes span four feet. During their rutting season, the elk will bugle loudly. Elk aren't native to this region, so my neighbors sure got a kick out of hearing the elk bugle in the fall.

The deer soon became quite popular with people from the area. Often hunters came by during hunting season to view my deer and take pictures. People not from such a culture sometimes don't understand that hunters live by a different standard and most often have a deep love for animals. Animals are raised and hunted for food, but they are also greatly enjoyed and respected. It's a more wild nature, and while my heart is soft for animals, I understand this natural code as well. And you can't buy meat any more organic than fresh venison.

One of my first deer was Uni. He eventually turned into a humongous white-tailed buck with a seventeen-point rack and one hundred seventy inches of horn. At first, he looked like a unicorn with his one horn—hence the name. As a unicorn deer and later because of his size and large rack, Uni was a showpiece in my tiny wild animal park.

Another favorite deer was Buckwheat. I raised him up from a fawn, and he turned into a twelve-pointer eventually. At about five years of age, he became really aggressive. Come the rut in September after he lost his velvet, Buckwheat was quite ornery in his quest to mate, seeing the other males—and everyone else—as threats to spar with.

One day in September, I came home early in the morning from Fairway Foods, formerly Carpenter Cook, after driving a semi all night on my usual graveyard shift. Penny was out on the porch getting ready to feed the deer before she went inside to cook breakfast. I offered to feed the deer and took the buckets to the deer enclosure.

The bucks had lost their velvet and were heading into the rut season, but I didn't think much of that this morning. After closing the gate, I walked in carrying two pails of corn, not really paying attention because I was so tired, when I heard Penny from the front porch.

"Look out!" she yelled.

I turned and faced Buckwheat.

His lips were rolled back, and he was sidestepping with his ears flat and making a wheezing sound that deer make when they're ready to fight. Buckwheat stared at me wildly like I was another buck invading his territory, not Buddy the guy who raised him from a fawn.

Before I could move, he came at me.

I dropped the pails of corn as he ran straight into each of the palms of my hands. The tines of his antlers dug into my skin. He lifted me up, and I flew into the air, landing on my back on the ground. He then pushed me about twenty to thirty feet as he tried getting his antlers into my gut like he'd do when fighting another deer. I'd never felt such strength in all my life, and I panicked.

My neighbor Bob Nichols just happened to pull into the yard at that moment. Bobby was about eighteen years old and lived five houses down. I'd called his family earlier that week asking to buy some cedar posts for my barnyard that housed our domestic animals. Bobby was dropping the posts off.

"Help him!" Penny screamed to Bobby, running toward the fence.

Buckwheat had me cornered and was ready to strike once again.

"Bobby, get a post and hit this deer over the head," I

shouted, trying to keep Buckwheat's horns from digging into my gut.

Bobby grabbed a post and raced inside the fence. He swung hard and knocked Buckwheat in the head. The deer acted dazed for a moment, but he released his hold.

"Don't hit him too hard," I shouted as I scampered to get up.

Buckwheat came right back at both of us. Bobby and I each grabbed an antler and pushed like two Green Bay Packers linemen as Buckwheat hammered hard, forcing us backward. We finally got loose and raced out of there.

My hands were bruised and bleeding. I doctored them up myself and sure thanked Bobby for showing up when he did.

This was Buckwheat's fifth set of antlers, and it made him fierce. When the kids came home from school or when anyone drove into the yard, he rammed the fence and tried inciting a fight.

Finally, I took rope and stood outside the enclosure. When he raced in to try ramming me through the fence, I wrapped that rope around his antlers and tied him up. Then I sawed his antlers off. They'd have fallen off in another month anyway, but taking his antlers took the wind out of Buckwheat's sails. He calmed down right away and gave us no more trouble that year.

But if Bobby hadn't stopped in when he did, I don't know what would have happened. Penny wasn't strong enough to contend with Buckwheat, and I wouldn't have wanted her to try anyway. White-tailed deer especially have enormous strength in their necks. Every year, deer farmers lose their lives during rut season.

Buckwheat taught me a valuable lesson: never take our history for granted and get comfortable.

Honeybear meeting some new friends in 1989. I was so excited at having my first bear!

CHAPTER NINE
Love of Bears

For years, I'd stop in at Henes Park to watch the bears. Henes Park is a large city park in Menominee, Michigan, running along the shoreline of Green Bay. It was filled with animals for the tourists to enjoy. Harvey and Sophie Inman were caretakers of the park.

I'd built the deer enclosures and obtained some animals from Harvey, but whenever I'd stop at the park, my longing for bears would grow. Harvey often let me visit with Teddy Bear, the old bear I eventually brought to the zoo many years later. The Inmans had all kinds of critters living at their house: raccoons, bobcats, and the bear cubs to name just a few.

In 1989, I received state licensing for a captive black bear. I heard about a bear breeder by West Bend, Wisconsin, and went down with Penny to pick out a little six-week-old black bear cub. We named her Honeybear.

This was my first big wild animal other than the deer,

and it was heaven having a baby black bear in the house. Penny nurtured it like a mommy bear would. I was still working long hours driving the semi, but Penny gave Honeybear all the care she needed. That bear became just like a dog running around the house.

When the kids went out to the school bus, Honeybear would follow. Then I'd let her out in the afternoon when the kids were coming home. Honeybear knew right where the kids got on and off the bus. She'd hide in the weeds and jump out when they came down the steps.

We became so accustomed to Honeybear that she was simply part of the family. We'd be eating supper, and that bear would eat off the table. It was no big deal until visitors would stop by and be shocked to discover a bear in the house. I'd have to ask people to check their pockets for any cigarettes or candy—Honeybear would rip the pockets right off your pants to get a treat.

After a while, people would just point us out. "Yeah, that's the DeYoungs. They have a bear living in the house with them."

One time Penny called really upset while I was in the middle of work.

"What's wrong?" I asked, worried something happened to one of the kids.

"Honeybear's breaking down the apple trees," she cried.

I told my foreman I had to leave and took off, getting home in about fifteen minutes. Sure enough, there was

Honeybear wreaking havoc in the orchard. She wasn't just yanking fruit off the branches; she was tearing down whole darn trees to get at the apples. Black bears do that in the wild, but these were Penny's favorite apple trees. Honeybear was over two hundred pounds at this time and a force to reckon with, if she wanted to be.

"Honeybear, come on," I called and ordered her back into her cage, where she went.

That was Honeybear. She never lacked in food. If she wanted something, she went and got it.

As Honeybear grew, it became time to get her some companions. Mike Krakowski built one of the first bear habitats at the zoo. Joe Krygoski donated poles and sent up his equipment for the job. Mike Brodzinski and Todd Powers, who are great at mason and concrete work, poured the concrete and did the floor for the swimming pool. Brothers Tommy and Rob Nemetz, excellent fabricators and welders, built a slider, the gates, and bear den.

Eventually, I met Ed and Pat Plemel. Ed was a Wisconsin captive wildlife breeder. He had bears and white-tailed deer. I went down there and brought home Coco and Boo-Boo, two chocolate-colored black bears. I really wanted these chocolates. Oh, they were so pretty.

Black bears come in five main colors—chocolate, cinnamon, blonde black, blue glacier, and the rare white—with crosses and color variations in between.

Honeybear was probably close to two years old when

I brought Coco and BooBoo home. She'd become cantankerous and played rough with the family. I got numerous stitches and scrapes, but we never declawed or defanged any of the bears. Since God made them that way to eat and defend themselves, I figured that was part of the game of having them. It was good for Honeybear to have other bears, though she certainly took the role of boss bear.

Over the years, our bear population continued to grow. We had a really good conservation officer, Wayne Coleman, from the Michigan Department of Resources. One February, Wayne got a call about a female cub found by the bay eating charcoal grease from an outdoor barbecue oven. The cub should've been denned up with her mom this time of year.

BUD DeYOUNG

Wayne headed out there and picked her up, but there was no mama bear around. Either the two were separated or something had happened to the mom. Wayne knew about my bears and gave me a call.

That little bear was in pretty poor shape when Wayne brought her to us. She was starving and needed lots of attention. This was our first rehab bear, and she didn't want our help at first. She was all paws and claws. (Most of my stitches over the years have been from black bears.) But with Penny's around-the-clock care and me helping all I could, it wasn't long before the little cub returned to health.

Since that first one, I've had numerous rescue bears. Many are found in town or have been hit by a car. We get our equipment and go see what we can do, then most often we release the animal back into the wild. We get at least two calls a year from our local animal control or law enforcement agencies to help with a wayward bear. It's rewarding to see the bear hightail it into the woods once he's set straight and patched up.

Honeybear lived a good life. She was feisty, and, with the other bears, she was always the first at the food bowl. She lived into her mid to late twenties. A bear's life span can be upwards into thirty years. Honeybear was part of our family for so long before we moved her into the bear habitat that everyone was sad at her passing, even though our family had changed dramatically in those years.

The number of bears that have come and gone over the decades since Honeybear is extensive. We've had about

twenty cubs born to us, and we've obtained bears and traded them to keep the genetics healthy and also to offer visitors a range of species to gain more knowledge about these amazing creatures.

The bears were my first real step toward other big animals. Before long, tigers would inhabit the property—with so much more to come.

We had a hard but good life. The kids grew up and started venturing into their own pursuits. I kept adding to our zoo and working at Fairway Foods six days a week, which still left a lot of work for Penny at home. The balancing act wasn't working out well.

After twenty years in upper Michigan, building a home in the woods, raising a family, and pursuing my love of people and animals, life was about to make a dramatic change. My passions would get to flourish, but they would come at a price.

PART TWO
The Price

Winters in the UP are always a challenge, and I spend all day just shoveling paths to get to each habitat to check on my critters, making sure they're safe and they have food and fresh water.

CHAPTER TEN
The Sign

Winter is now upon us at the zoo. I count the days until we open.

The seasons are more difficult to predict with global warming. Last winter was uncommonly mild. Spring came early, but in the summer, we had a shocking heat wave in July that kept our visitors away.

In the autumn, the animals tried to prepare us for the coming cold. The bears stopped eating sooner and settled into their dens earlier than expected. The arctic foxes turned snow-white while last year they never fully turned from their summer coats of black. The snowshoe hares turned pure white as well. I saw the signs, and in the autumn we were preparing.

Then the weather deceived us. An early snowstorm in October had us rushing to bring the exotics inside. It seemed Indian summer had been skipped altogether, but then on Thanksgiving Day, it was an unbelievable fifty-five degrees. I remember Thanksgivings in the late eighties and nineties when it was ten degrees below zero and the snow was almost up to our waists.

Even into December, we had sunny days in the mid to high forties. I took every day as a gift, as it meant one less day of winter. Chores are easier without numb fingers, frozen water and ponds, and every extremity bundled up.

Then right before Christmas, a major blizzard swept in. The roads were closed, and people hunkered down inside to wait it out. We had everything buttoned up. The critters were warm and snug in their many shelters, but Carrie and I faced the weather to do our rounds at the zoo and the animal rescue.

The power went out, and in a storm like that, I knew it would be a while before it came back on. I ventured into the blinding snow, driving to town for extra gas for the generators.

Carrie's father put in a bypass system so when we lose power, we throw a switch and start up the generators to ensure that all our reptiles, exotics, and Wallace are safe from the cold. We also have our huge woodstoves to keep us warm and for cooking.

On a few of those nights, Carrie stayed at the rescue to keep a closer eye on some of the recovering animals. I missed her and wished she were here; I'm not the best at sharing, I suppose.

But at least Louie keeps me company. He can be kind

and loving in a way not even a dog can be. I enjoy it, knowing our time is limited till the day he is ready to move into the primate habitat with others of his kind.

Calls come in from local ranches for me to pick up cows with ice-related injuries, pneumonia, and such. When it's not much over twenty degrees in the day, we have an endless supply of beef for the big cats.

This is the face of winter. It's harsh and grueling, but I sometimes pause to remember that these are the challenges of living my dream.

Life has a way of sidetracking people from the childhood passions we're probably all born with and often forget as we go on through the years.

When Penny and I married, I moved from the suburban life to the country, just as I'd dreamed. I jumped into having a family of my own, which set me on another path that was full of love and rewards and also hard work. Perhaps it wouldn't have been all consuming without my father-in-law's prodding and my own workaholic tendencies, but the time passed like a blur with much of it devoured by wearisome labor that paid the bills but did little to feed my passion for animals.

After I left my little backyard zoo in Indiana, those childhood dreams never disappeared. They were just buried beneath a mountain of responsibility and work.

We had critters at our place, but I wanted an area

that would allow people to visit, see, and enjoy animals. I wanted to share how amazing they could be with people who didn't normally get the chance to be around them.

For some, this might sound like a strange dream. But for as long as I could remember, I was fascinated and attracted to the animal kingdom and sharing it with others. I'd spent countless hours studying and enjoying creatures of every kind, species, size, and type. I watched how they ate, what they ate, how they moved, and the ways they interacted with others from their species.

The only word that described it was *passion*. And passion seems to choose us instead of us choosing it.

I lived where I wanted, had a great family, and with Penny, I had built something nice. I worked my butt off and did what was needed of me. That was all right for a time. But it wasn't that old dream, not quite.

The saying from the movie *Field of Dreams* about *if you build it, they will come* was certainly true for my little zoo. I built it bit by bit over the years with collected wire, then larger gates and buildings and habitats.

First, I had the deer, followed by the bear cubs and wolves and then the tigers. And people kept coming to see the animals.

Six nights a week, I still drove the semi. Then I'd come home and work on the zoo, caring for my animals during the day. I didn't have time for much sleep, but I didn't care. This was my passion. The work I did at the grocery supply warehouse provided for the family and built my fledgling wildlife park.

I was a multitasking machine. I still am today. For ten to fifteen years, I was doing four to five jobs every day.

Throughout the warm months, people visited the animals as word of them spread around the area. I loved interacting with visitors, sharing my knowledge and stories of each animal. It was like my childhood backyard collection—only bigger and with more people.

I didn't know how long I could balance it all. There were moments when I wanted to give something up, but of course, I couldn't quit the job that supported my family.

My semi driving job was more than just a place to put in hours. Over the years, I'd made good friends with the owners and my coworkers. When I drove, I met people all over the Upper Peninsula who became my friends. I'd inherited my people skills from my parents.

Invariably I'd talk about the animals already around the house—our bears, deer, and the other critters. Here and there people would donate supplies, outdated produce, and other feed, and that helped immensely. Sometimes they'd come to view the animals.

Though I'd moved back into pursuing my passion, it wore on me, and there were times when I wondered if I should give up the zoo dream for a while longer.

People get signs in their lives pointing the way they should go. Sometimes it's a confirmation that you're moving in the right direction. I received a sign that was about as literal and in your face as it could possibly be.

Uncle George came up from Whiting, Indiana, for a visit. From inside his car, he pulled out a painted sign that said DeYoung Family Zoo. Something about seeing the words on that sign struck me hard. That was exactly what I wanted: a family zoo.

Uncle George and I went out to the end of the road and attached the sign to a post at the entrance of our driveway. It was real to me then. And the decision to move forward and build a family zoo became my burning desire. Today that same sign remains at the entrance of the parking lot.

At the age of about thirty-five, I finally grew a backbone and stopped putting off my dream. With renewed vision, I was confident that I'd eventually retire from driving a truck and do the zoo full-time. That seemed like a pipe dream, but I stopped fooling myself that I'd be content with the crazy juggling of everything, not giving 100 percent of myself to any of it.

It didn't happen overnight. But now my focus was unwavering.

One of the greatest myths is that cats don't like water, but I can tell you this: they love the snow! It's great fun watching our tigers run and play in all that white stuff!

CHAPTER ELEVEN
Winter's Sting

The winter days are mapped out and gauged by the temperature outside. The calendar tracks how many days until we open again.

My major focus for the six months of winter is the care of the animals: warmth if needed; fresh food, including meat, grains, and hay; clean housing; and fresh water. The water can be the most challenging with freezing temperatures that require me to break the ice from the ponds and troughs of dozens of habitats every day. In addition, the critters need to be kept in clean and comfortable environments, a daunting task in the cold.

Firewood becomes part of the challenge. I have two outdoor wood burners that Carrie's dad, Bart, hooked up. They are huge stoves that keep everything warm, including our house, the other outbuildings, and Wallace's hippo habitat.

I'm outside much of the day. My schedule doesn't revolve around zoo shows, as it does in the summer, but around chores and more chores.

Fill the woodstoves.

Pick up the meat when local ranchers call (often several a day).

Cut up the beef.

Thaw the water for the animals.

Feed the animals.

Clean the habitats.

Completely clean Wallace's indoor pond at least weekly.

Be sure every animal has continued access to its shelter.

Watch the trees after every storm, and keep them trimmed throughout the year.

Since my first winter in the Upper Peninsula, I've experienced the arctic storms that drop in every year, beating their frigid winds, rain, and snow onto the earth without mercy. They happen during the months when the bears are smart enough to slumber and live off their own fat. I wish to be as smart as those bears.

When the cold settles in hard and deep, I turn into a complainer. Every chore that I sail through in the warmer months is now a strain and a challenge. The basics, like stepping outside my door, require effort. It's a frozen world. My fingers fight the numbness, and now my knuckles ache with arthritis. Our equipment must be maintained to fight the cold. Vehicles require antifreeze, and I wish everything at the zoo including myself had a similar antifreeze elixir.

BUD DeYOUNG

Every year, I swear that I'll make changes before next year. Changes that will make winter less taxing. I'll find more help; I'll enclose the area where I cut those huge slabs of beef; I'll chop the firewood sooner; I'll get the income that will make these months less stressful. The dream needs management. I'm still working on that.

As my kids grew up and left home, my marriage started going down the tubes. My interest was in the zoo, and Penny wanted different things in life. The zoo grew up around us. I still worked nights driving truck for Fairway Foods. In the daytime, I managed the animals.

Our finances were pretty stable with my many jobs. But I was wearing out from the years of work and little sleep. As the kids moved out and were no longer eligible for my insurance plan, it became less and less necessary for me to keep driving a truck. I was spread too thin and for little return.

Penny and I argued a lot, and at times, I looked at her as if she were a stranger. I'm sure she felt the same about me. We'd lived all those years together, working toward the goal of raising a family, but now we didn't have much in common or seem to know how to talk.

We were married for twenty years. In that time, we had built a home on our forty acres, our children had grown up, and our animals had come and some had gone.

Penny was a great mother and homemaker. She put up

with my animals in the house and her little ranch being turned into a zoo, habitat by habitat. I suppose some women wouldn't allow a bear to eat with the family at dinner or animals to crowd the rooms of her house even more than our children and the many kids who stayed with us.

Penny was more of an introvert than me, and as the zoo grew and people filled the grounds every summer and visited throughout the year, she started to withdraw. The reality of a zoo in and around our small home, well, I think it was too much for her.

But in the end, I take the blame for our undoing. When I have a vision, there isn't much that can stop me. That can be good, but at times, I've hurt people along the way. In the moment, sometimes it's hard to see what's happening. I did wrong by Penny. We drifted apart, but then I really drifted.

Kristen was young, beautiful, and as passionate about the zoo as I was. My marriage to Penny was like two people working together to perform our separate duties. Kristen woke me up to what a relationship could be, or seemed like it could be, and I was hooked.

Penny moved off the property. She didn't want the responsibility of the animals, and the zoo wasn't her dream. When she left, the kids went to her. Our youngest, Becky, had graduated high school, and Carry and Brad were already in college. I couldn't blame them. After all, Penny had been there, tending them as they grew up and

BUD DeYOUNG

helping them through those rough junior high and high school patches.

I was the bad guy. I was the one who ended it. Penny was a fabulous mom and raised wonderful kids. She worked hard, cared for our home, and was a good wife. In the end, it didn't work out and life went on.

What else can we do but move forward when things fall apart, either by our own hand or the choice of another?

Kristen and I married fast. It wouldn't be long before she was gone.

With me driving the truck, Kristen was at the house, tending to the animals, but she wasn't really animal oriented the way I'd first believed. To survive this kind of life, you need that and much more.

There were a lot of factors, but the result was a man alone with his animals. Maybe I was living a clichéd country-western song, but that whole thing really knocked my boots out from under me.

My life with Penny and the kids and building our place was over. Then the new marriage had fallen apart. I took responsibility, but finding my bearings in the aftermath took time.

For the next year, I nursed my wounds. My animals were a comfort. There's nothing like a dog to cure the blues, and I had plenty of dogs, wolves, bears, and deer. But Luna, Kristen's German shepherd mix that she left behind, was a particular comfort. Luna slept with me and was my sidekick as I became reclusive.

I kept busy with my love of animals and my outside job, but I steered clear of women.

Yet painful experiences can push us to take risks we wouldn't normally take. They can prod us beyond our norm, off the beaten path, and into the dream we've danced around or kept hidden inside.

The losses hadn't crushed me, even if sometimes it felt like it. One day, I knew it was time.

At last, my life's work went completely to the animals.

 BUD DeYOUNG

CHAPTER TWELVE
The Big Step Out

While we don't get a lot of cash donations, especially in the winter, we're gifted with donations of food for the animals.

Angeli Foods is our biggest donor, providing outdated lettuce and other produce several times a week. This keeps Wallace the hippo and many of our other animals full throughout the year.

As before, ranches all over the region still call us to remove cattle that have died due to weather, injury, or age. It saves them money from paying one of the packinghouses to remove the animal, and it provides fresh meat for the big cats.

This week, Great Lakes Foods (formerly Fairway Foods and before that Carpenter Cook) has donated some post-dated produce to the zoo, as they do when they can. I drive down, pick up the produce, talk about old times with my friends, and thank them for the donation. They've helped me greatly over the years.

As I drive away from the warehouse, I remember the day I gave my final notice. The response from my foreman, vice president, and then president were unanimous: "Oh no, you can't leave yet."

They reminded me that I had less than a year before getting a pension and benefits with retirement.

But I had hit the wall.

The hours were long. Then I came home to more chores than ever, and I wanted to spend time with the animals. My double whammy divorces stripped my finances. I didn't have children and a wife to come home to, but that also meant they didn't need supporting, either.

Much of my life was in the crapper. Then it struck me: it was just me and the critters. I was ready to experience my dream not as a side project but as my whole life.

I'd worked the same job a total of nineteen years and six months. All I needed was a little more time, but those months loomed larger than life, and I was completely worn-out.

I told my bosses that it would be unfair to them and to my animals for me to stay. When I was out on the road, I spent most of my time thinking about the zoo. At the zoo, I was exhausted from driving and couldn't give my animals all the attention I wanted. I'd surely make a mistake in one area or the other if I didn't make a change.

Their response amazed me. They supported me by saying that if my heart was at home with my animals, then that's where I needed to be. I left with their blessings.

I love those guys—Jerry Van and Ben Stewart and all the rest at Great Lakes. I have no regrets from my years there, and I appreciate what they've done for me both during the time I worked and in the help they've provided ever since. We've remained good friends.

After I resigned, my animals never wanted for anything. But while they came first, I nearly starved for three or four years as I learned how to manage a business. I went from having a regular income to trying to make it off the zoo's income. I supplemented as needed by working in the woods, cutting firewood and cedar post.

I woke early, ready for a long day of chores, scooping poop, feeding critters, cutting firewood, mending or building fences, caring for injured animals, and enjoying my time with them.

I loved it!

At last, my full attention and strength were put into my animals. I'd spent decades learning from others, studying and building knowledge on everything from animal habits and instincts to the best types of enclosures for various species and safety precautions for acres with multiple creatures.

It didn't seem real at first. But I had the time to let this life grow around me. It was a new start. I discovered that second chances often bring the best things in life. For me, that included a woman who changed my world completely.

BUD DeYOUNG

CHAPTER THIRTEEN
Big Cat Carrie

The rescue ranch is taking in thirty horses.

Thirty.

The horses are in very bad shape. Owned by two hoarders, the animals were basically left in the pasture to starve, dehydrate, and suffer in the weather.

The vet says that not all will survive. Carrie is furious, heartbroken, and determined to save as many as possible. She's pulling in every bit of help she can find, and I'm taking over at the zoo so she can focus her energy at the ranch.

Carrie's going through hay like crazy, even with the huge rounds I unloaded just a few months ago. But I didn't suggest that thirty horses might be more than the rescue can manage with all the other domestic animals it's housing. I know Carrie, and there'd be no point. She's just as stubborn and passionate as me.

During the years of moving beyond my double divorces, I dated this girl or that, but there was nothing serious or long-term.

The guys in town took notice of "Buddy's girls," as they called them. They had a saying: "As soon as Buddy throws the wood in the stove; they're gone." And that wasn't far from the truth. The summer attracted them. It was glamour, if you can call a zoo glamorous. There was excitement with the daily visitors, the tours, and the animals. Then the weather turned, and it was time to stoke up the woodstove. Snow locked us in, and the chores became a daily challenge. Every year, by the fall or winter, I was alone with my animals.

Then along came a yellow-haired beauty.

In the fall of 2003, Carrie visited the zoo. Her best friend, Dereck Renier, had a cabin in Faithorn, Michigan, and they were going up with friends from Green Bay, Wisconsin, about an hour away. One of the routine stops that Carrie forced upon the others was the zoo. They'd been doing that for years.

Carrie was very enthused about the animals, and she enjoyed sharing them with her friends, even when it was obvious they were anxious to leave. They had to drag her away every time they came.

On this trip, Carrie was visiting with Dereck's mom for a girls' weekend at the cabin.

I recognized her, as I do many a person, thinking, *Yep,*

BUD DeYOUNG

that's the girl from Green Bay. Someone who really loves the critters. She was especially fond of the alligators. The guys never wanted anything to do with the gators, but the girl from Green Bay was always holding them or the snakes.

This time, I finally learned her name, because I asked. And I learned she worked as a preschool teacher in Green Bay.

After talking to Carrie and hearing just how long she'd been coming by the zoo, I said, "Well, if you have any free time from your job, come up and give me a hand."

This was October, when I had little help after the teenagers and college-aged volunteers went back to school.

Carrie said she would, but I figured, *Hell, I'll never hear from her again.*

Less than a week later, Carrie called and asked if I needed a hand.

I never turn away help, and there was no doubt in my mind that she liked animals. Immediately, I saw how gifted she was with them. And she was beautiful, smart, and seemed to be a nice person. I was attracted right away.

That first day together was quite memorable. I didn't want to stop talking to her. She had so many ideas and was full of passion for animals, for the children she taught, and for life. We didn't want to leave each other; at least I didn't want her to go. Yet as she drove away, I couldn't be sure she'd return. But Carrie kept making the long drive from Green Bay to help with the animals.

I stopped by her school a few times and was amazed at

how she taught her kids about different languages, planets, and other things above and beyond the usual lessons. Education was important to her, and she was very good at her job. And just like the animals, the kids adored Carrie.

As she came up more and more to help me, our feelings continued to grow. After about six months, Carrie started staying at the zoo with me, even during the week. It was tough on her. She'd leave so early in the morning to be at the school at 6:30 a.m. and even earlier during the winter months.

The guys' saying about Buddy's girls leaving when I tossed the wood into the stove didn't apply to Carrie. I tossed the wood in, but she didn't leave. The snow came and left, and Carrie worked her ass off alongside me.

It wasn't till months later that we were at dinner with friends and some comment about age fell into the conversation.

"How old do you think I am?" Carrie asked with sass in her voice.

I hadn't given it much thought, to be honest. Perhaps I think of myself as younger than I am, but while our age gap was evident, it didn't seem particularly shocking to me.

I shrugged. "Thirty-one, thirty-two?"

Her eyes grew wide enough to let me know that I was dead wrong.

"Go on and tell me," I said, unwilling to make another guess.

"I just turned twenty-four," she said with her arms crossed.

That took me aback. I was fifty-one. Every one of my children is older than Carrie. Our age difference is twenty-seven years.

"Well, I thought you looked good for your age," I said with a nervous laugh. "Damn," I muttered. What else could I say?

Much like mine, Carrie's background with animals stems from her love of them. She started with cats and then added guinea pigs, frogs, fish—all the small pet shop varieties. She read everything she could find about them. As a pet owner, Carrie was into proper diets and animal health. Then she started helping people with their animals—babysitting, walking, and working with various breeds and species. When she'd hear of someone having problems with a pet or an animal's diet, she'd dive into researching the issue and then offer advice. People started coming to her for help.

Her passion brought her to the DeYoung Family Zoo.

As Carrie and I grew closer, she became a partner instead of a helper. Her nurturing touch with the animals, especially the babies and injured ones, astounded me.

Carrie was full of fresh ideas on how to make the zoo work better, grow larger, and bring more of an educational aspect to the program. I was an old dog, and, though I talked about improvements, sometimes I dug my heels in when she wanted to implement her plans.

Over the first couple of years, we butted heads a lot—and I mean a lot—but once I considered her idea, the majority of the time I realized it was pretty good.

I'd say, "Why don't we do this?"

She'd say, "That was my idea in the first place."

That happened about a hundred times.

Carrie and I have a unique relationship. We make each other and the zoo better by our bickering. We are similar in that we're hardheaded, opinionated, independent thinkers, stubborn, and quite vocal.

Our differences make us clash as much as our similarities. I'm old-school, spontaneous, and could sit around telling stories till the night turned cold. Carrie is always coming up with new ideas and keeps us straight with rules and regulations.

Other couples couldn't handle the way we bicker, but it works for us. We don't hold these arguments against each other. We understand that we make each other better, and at the end of the day, our love is deep and lasting.

With us together, my zoo grew by leaps and bounds.

The ideas Carrie initiated brought great changes. The first was the educational aspect. We started doing shows to teach visitors about the different animals and to spread the message of conservation.

Conservation is about preserving, protecting, and restoring the natural environment and wildlife. By

BUD DeYOUNG

introducing our visitors to both native and exotic wild-life and giving talks about their unique qualities and behaviors, we hoped to bring better understanding and help to endangered creatures and animals of every kind. When a person gets close to a critter and understands it, they usually don't see animals the same afterward.

Carrie also designed an itinerary of shows for the visitors to see during the day: bear feeding, canine shows, big-cat feeding, reptile encounters, alligator shows on the weekends, and baby encounters. The presentations became very popular.

Carrie with one of the lions during the daily Big Cat Feeding time where visitors get a firsthand look at the liveliness of our cats as they get fresh butchered meat. It's a huge hit with everyone!

In addition to her educational input, Carrie had great ideas about building different habitats. But she wanted to dive in right now, which didn't work into the finances. She wanted to expand faster than our means could handle. Occasionally I had to rein her in.

One of the first habitats we built together was for the mountain lions. My longtime friend Fred Reidell brought out stone and his giant excavator to help with landscaping, creating the dens, and building a water system. Carrie wanted to include a waterfall, or royal waters, as we call it, for the cats to enjoy.

Carrie had specific ideas about that habitat. Again, we butted heads all the way through this first major project, but once it was finished, we were extremely proud of it.

Another development we completed was to section off the zoo into different trails: the North American Trail, African Trail, and Asian Trail, with the habitats of animals native to these regions found down each one.

Then Carrie's dad started coming up. Bart is a genius of a building contractor. His ideas are phenomenal and have really improved the place.

Carrie's brother became an asset too. Hayden has been coming to the zoo since he was just a young kid. Carrie would drive down and pick him up. Those few visits and sleepovers turned into every weekend and all summer long. He dedicated himself to what Carrie and I are passionate about. Now he has his license and drives up on weekends through the winter to give us a hand when we don't have much help.

Dereck Renier, Carrie's longtime best friend, is also practically family. During the summer, he stays in a trailer by the hyenas. Throughout many winters, he lives at the zoo during the week and provides invaluable help with the daily chores.

I was already in the process of growing the zoo when Carrie came, but her connections and ideas boosted my efforts. She propelled my place into what it is today with our ideas never ending. I love her for many reasons, such as her gift and passion for animals, her amazing heart, and how she nurtures both people and critters. Another big reason is for what she has done for the zoo and for me.

Discovering someone with a similar passion changed everything. With Carrie, my vision for the zoo expanded beyond my original dream. We developed some of my plans more quickly, implemented some of Carrie's, and became a more professional zoo with many new exotic and native animals. And there was much more, beyond either of our dreams, to come.

Contrary to popular belief, some cats love water. And if you don't believe me, then wait until you hear what Kenya did.

CHAPTER FOURTEEN
Mishaps and Learning Curves

I am sitting in the ER getting stitches.

Usually, I patch myself up and save the time and the money. But this incident required a hospital trip.

In trying to beat some bad weather coming in, I was building a nest inside the black panther exhibit so the young cat would have a better place to sleep. The leopard didn't mind me in there on the ladder. Carrie told me not to do it, but I ignored her. I won't live it down for a while. Dereck was helping with the project, standing outside the pen as my spotter, watching my back in case the leopard became agitated by my presence.

The ladder under me didn't have grippers on the bottom. I reached up, and suddenly the whole ladder slid right out from under me. The gate latch skewered my arm, and I hit the ground with my knee first, then my rib cage.

The leopard watched me writhing in pain on the ground, but he didn't react. Dereck jumped in quick, grabbed my shirt, and pulled me out. He then called Carrie and drove me to the ER.

The doc is giving me both interior and exterior stitches under my arm. I also broke a rib. One knee is pretty sore as well. This is not what I needed.

We've had mishaps and learning experiences over the years. Just as with raising kids, you can't work with animals without some surprises along the way.

I don't worry about animals escaping. That's one crisis we'll never have. Sometimes my mind goes into overdrive thinking of potential scenarios that might cause problems. Then I do something about them, going beyond what's required. For example, we have double-walled, electric fencing around the habitats, which isn't required by government regulations. However, it is required for my peace of mind. With it, I'm confident that we'll never have an escapee.

Yet there are all kinds of other stories to tell.

CATS DON'T LIKE WATER?

Many of my first animals, like Honeybear the black bear cub, grew up alongside my kids. Kenya, our first lion cub, was one of those critters. Kenya spent a lot of time in the house before we rescued a cub named Nala and moved them into the new lion habitat.

But when he was still a cub, Kenya came inside the house quite often. He acted completely at home, similar to a domestic cat, just much stronger and with bigger claws and teeth.

One day I was working in the basement when water started running down the stairs from the main floor.

"What the hell?" I said, wondering if a pipe had broken or if someone had left a faucet on. I yelled for Penny or the kids but didn't get an answer, so I raced upstairs through the water and followed the liquid trail to Becky's room.

When I peered inside, I saw Kenya.

That lion looked up from Becky's water bed, where he was stretched out and splashing water all over the damn place. He'd poked holes in the mattress with his claws. Lions usually don't like water, but Kenya was having a great time in it.

I hadn't realized those water beds held so much water. Kenya created quite a mess. The carpet and water bed were ruined, and we had a job cleaning everything up. I don't think we had another water bed in the house again. This was just another day in the lives of the DeYoung family.

A PLOTTING PARROT

A short time before Carrie came to the zoo, I'd taken in a beautiful green-winged macaw named Kiwi. He didn't like many people, but after Carrie spent time with him, Kiwi warmed up to her.

Eventually, Carrie was able to hold Kiwi and carry him around. He'd sit at the table and eat spaghetti off her plate.

According to Carrie, parrots love pasta as long as it's with marinara, not Alfredo, sauce. We made Kiwi's home in his great big cage in our kitchen.

Kiwi became an important part of Carrie's everyday life. He woke with her on those mornings Carrie got up early to drive to Green Bay to teach.

When it was time to wake me before she left for the day, Carrie would set Kiwi at the end of the bed. He'd dive under the blankets and walk all the way up the bed under the covers until he got right next to my face on the pillow. Then he'd shake his head and say, "Hello! Hello!"

He'd do that until I'd wake and grumble, "Hello, Kiwi."

Then Kiwi would climb onto the bedpost and start dancing as if quite proud of himself. I'd pull myself out of bed, and Kiwi would come eat breakfast with me. Carrie stood there laughing at the entire daily routine.

Kiwi was one of those fun animals, because he was not only beautiful but he could also talk back. He had a pretty good vocabulary.

Carrie integrated Kiwi into the shows at the zoo. She'd stand in the crowd with Kiwi on her arm, and he'd do flips and turns, take things out of Carrie's hands, and talk to the visitors.

One year, we were raising a baby mountain lion named Cyrus. Cyrus was Carrie's baby. She has a soft spot for cougars, the only big cats that purr.

The cougar had free rein of the house as usual. When

it came time to give him his bottle or to play, Carrie would call Cyrus by making cougar sounds—a sort of gentle and friendly growl.

One afternoon, Carrie was doing housework and ran downstairs to change out the laundry. As she worked, she heard a thud and the quick padded steps of the cougar as he ran from the living room into the kitchen. Then the sound stopped. After a pause, Carrie heard Cyrus's slow walk back to the living room where he hopped onto the couch.

A moment later, Carrie again heard the thuds of Cyrus jumping off the couch and running from the living room to the kitchen. Then the sound stopped. This happened three times.

Carrie was concerned now, wondering what Cyrus was doing, what he had, or what he was after. She finished the laundry in a hurry.

As she raced up the basement stairs, Carrie heard the sound of an older cougar coming from the kitchen. She froze, considering what it could be.

Carrie came through the door. The only thing in the kitchen was Kiwi.

Kiwi had been imitating the cougar sound that Carrie makes to call Cyrus. The young cougar would then run into the kitchen looking for Mom, thinking, *Mom's going to feed me or give me some attention.* When Mom wasn't there, Cyrus would head back to the living room and his cozy spot on the couch. As soon as Cyrus got comfortable again, Kiwi would make the sound, and the cougar would run back in.

That bird was so smart. He was messing with Cyrus.

Carrie caught him in the act. "Kiwi, you're busted," she said in a scolding tone, trying not to laugh.

Kiwi raised a wing and tucked his head under. He knew he was being mischievous.

We were pretty amazed by the whole event.

But one problem for Kiwi was that little by little Carrie had less time for him. She was home with him all summer, then the rest of the year, she worked at both the zoo and the preschool in Green Bay, driving over an hour each way. She worked long hours, so she'd leave early after chores, then get home and do some of the evening chores.

Kiwi started displaying characteristics of depression. He plucked at his feathers and squawked and grew upset because he didn't get to spend time with her.

Carrie decided that the best solution was to get Kiwi a girlfriend. Her name was Mango. She was a beautiful blue-and-gold macaw.

Kiwi and Mango absolutely loved each other.

However, once Kiwi fell for his new girl, he no longer cared much for Carrie. It was a good thing for Kiwi but bad for Carrie.

We've experienced it a hundred times. There comes a point when we do what's best for the animal. But one of the hard parts of the zoo is that while we get attached to certain animals, eventually they move on without us. It's a proud moment, but it's never easy. Carrie learned that with Kiwi.

HUGGY BEAR AND MISSING TEETH

Huggy Bear was the first bear Carrie and I raised together. We brought him home during the winter when baby bears are born.

This was the first black bear that I'd raised in many

years, and I was pretty excited about it. Huggy Bear was so cute. Just this tiny, teddy bear–sized cub with big brown eyes. He'd pout his little lips when he'd smell or talk. Each of us spent a lot of one-on-one time with him. When he was inside the house, Huggy liked crawling into laundry baskets and being pulled around. He'd also hang on our sides or backs and go with us wherever we went.

We took care of Huggy Bear like a mama bear would. And like most babies

Meet Huggy Bear—master home decorator and part-time dentist.

at the zoo, Huggy had the run of the house.

In the first years when Carrie moved in, we had a living room and bedrooms. Now, except for our bedroom, the rooms have been turned into an animal nursery, hospital, and critter-housing complex.

But back then, the larger baby animals generally enjoyed sleeping on the couch in the living room. We didn't have many animals inside when Huggy Bear arrived, because it was winter and most of the animals are born in the spring. In the early spring, the house is often full of babies if the mothers need help, if people bring rescues by, or if the weather is still too cold for newborns to be outside.

One evening I came home, exhausted from the day, and Huggy raced to greet me. I said hello, picked him up by the scruff, gave him a kiss, and then put him down. I flipped on the TV and settled onto the couch for a little nap before completing evening chores. Carrie was in the kitchen making dinner, and Huggy Bear kept running around all full of energy, chasing Zech the Chihuahua and prodding me to play with him.

"Come on. Papa Bear doesn't want to play," I grumbled, shooing him away.

Carrie called Huggy into the kitchen and gave him some grapes to distract him so I could rest.

No sooner had I drifted off than something hit like a sledgehammer into my face and stomach. I shouted at the top of my lungs, and Huggy was on my lap screaming at the top of his lungs. He took off running for Carrie.

My mouth was throbbing, and I tasted blood. A huge framed painting that had been on the wall above the couch had crashed onto the floor.

Carrie raced into the room with Huggy Bear attached to her legs. "Where are your teeth?" she shouted.

I touched my mouth. My two front teeth were gone.

While I had dozed off, Huggy had climbed up the couch and stood on his two legs to reach for the framed picture. He'd lost his balance and pulled the painting down with him. While he had landed on my stomach, the corner of the frame had smashed out my front teeth.

Soon afterward, Carrie and I moved the TV into our bedroom, replaced the couch with built-in pens for animals, and saw the end of framed art in our house. Our living and breathing art was more than enough, we figured.

As for Huggy Bear, he quickly got over my scaring the life out of him, and I forgave him for a painful trip to the dentist.

EQUIPMENT FAILURE

My neighbor Tom Rivard has helped me out of some near disasters.

We became friends years ago when he was building his house across the road. When he was digging his basement, Tom pulled out several huge rocks that he kept in the driveway—until his son nearly smashed his truck on them.

Tom donated the boulders for the grizzly habitat. They were so large I had to hire someone to move them over.

One spring, I was driving my tractor across the tiger pond. I do this all winter long, hauling firewood around the place. The ponds are frozen solid for half the year. But the pond had thawed more than I realized, and the front end of my tractor plummeted through the ice. I tried putting her in reverse as the water covered the front half of the tractor. It was stuck.

I headed over to Tom's house and told him what happened. He got a good laugh, then brought his tractor over. He pulled up on a rock, tied a rope to my tractor, and slowly moved backward. We weren't sure it was going to work, but inch by inch, we eventually got it out. If not for Tom, the tractor would've stayed there all summer until the heat shrank the pond.

When you constantly work a tractor on your own land, it's easy to push the limit too far. This wasn't the first time. One very frigid December day, I was out hauling firewood with the tractor. I made it across the creek just fine, cut a bunch of wood, and loaded the bucket down. The wood was green, not dried by the seasons, so heavier than most firewood. As I drove back across the creek, the weight sank the tractor into the soft sand and gravel, and I was stuck.

I needed to get the tractor out for two reasons. First, I needed that firewood. Second, if the creek kept rising, I could lose the tractor altogether. Tom and his rig came to pull me out again.

Neighbors like that are like gold.

Tom likes to shake his head at me, commenting on how even in the coldest days of winter, when it's twenty below with high winds, he still sees me outside cutting up beef for the cats to eat. He sees my lights on at ten at night as I'm still working.

I shrug and say that's what it takes to run a zoo in the Upper Peninsula. But it also takes good people like Tom helping out when I need a hand.

RABBIT WINS AND LOSSES

The first spring we were together, I took Carrie to her first animal swap. I'd been telling her stories all winter about the swaps and sales that I'd attended as a teenager with George Dragic where people who raised animals brought their extra critters to buy, sell, trade, swap bloodlines, and things like that.

We were both excited to attend one. This was the first time we'd gone anywhere together, and getting to share something I'd loved since childhood was pretty exciting as well. Carrie loved it, just as I expected.

For hours, we walked the rows and rows that displayed unique breeds of animals. The people enjoyed Carrie's questions and her compliments about how beautiful the animals were. She was amazed by their vast knowledge of the specific breeds of animals they were raising.

Carrie especially liked the rabbits. She'd had a pet rabbit named Snarfer when she moved into her first place. The Holland Lop rabbit was litter box trained and would sit on the couch and eat carrots with her. Snarfer would even curl up with her cats, she said.

Carrie wanted to get a couple of rabbits at the swap, and I thought this was a great way for her to learn how to bid during the auction.

At first, I did the bidding to show her how it was done. Then I turned it over to Carrie. There was a beautiful Lionhead rabbit up for bid, a brand-new breed at the time, and we knew that no one had heard of this kind of rabbit in the Upper Peninsula. Each little rabbit had a fuzzy tuft of hair around its head like a lion; they were unique and beautiful in a variety of colors.

I started going over the possibilities. We could get a number of those Lionhead rabbits, breed them, and sell them to locals. It would be a fun side project for the two of us, and it reminded me a little of how my brother and I had raised pigeons in Highland, Indiana.

Carrie started bidding, and I stood behind her, telling her to go, stop, or keep bidding.

This one guy seemed set on bidding against her. After we lost several of the rabbits I wanted, my temper flared. I wasn't letting that guy get any more of our rabbits.

As the next ones came up, I poked Carrie to keep bidding. An excitement came over me with the idea of these beautiful rabbits and the fact that we were starting a new little adventure together.

We'd gone there to buy a lot of other animals, but when it was done, I stood back a little stunned.

We'd spent nine hundred dollars on rabbits.

I couldn't believe how many I'd bought and for such prices. It was unheard of. But the eagerness to get those animals and share them with Carrie took over my normal logic.

The two of us loaded the truck with our rabbits and just a handful of other animals, and we drove home.

When we got to the zoo, a few volunteers came up to the truck to see what we'd brought home. Their mouths dropped when I opened the truck and it was almost completely full of rabbits. But then they looked at those little Lionheads, all white fur with blue eyes. They were the most beautiful rabbits any of us had ever seen.

We had a little area by the petting zoo where Carrie and I spent an entire day building and fixing up a spot for the rabbits. I taught Carrie how to put the cages together and build hutches. She was so excited by it all because she just loved those rabbits. We laughed and smiled while I told her stories about my childhood critters. It was a great time together.

As we worked, a few people came by and admired how beautiful the rabbits were. They had the softest fur. Finally, we were all set up and could settle the bunnies inside their new home. Several of the does were pregnant when we bought them, so we anticipated baby bunnies in the coming weeks.

A few days later, Carrie went out and a couple of the rabbits were missing. We looked around and couldn't figure out how they had escaped or what had happened.

The next morning, she came in upset, carrying a dead rabbit. I felt bad, mainly for Carrie. Though hard, this happens.

The next day, Carrie went out to check on the rabbits and came running back. She was bawling so hard that I could hardly understand her. I raced out to the petting zoo and couldn't believe my eyes. Every single rabbit was dead. Carrie was freaking out, and I was just stunned.

I thought of the dead rabbit from the day before and asked Carrie if she'd had a chance to inspect it. She'd been too upset and just wanted to get it away from the other bunnies.

As I looked at all our beautiful dead rabbits, I saw the signs that they'd been killed by a weasel. The first rabbits were his way of testing things out. Then he'd come back and killed the rest.

We had spent way too much money and all that time on those beautiful Lionhead bunnies, and every single one was gone.

Carrie was crushed, and I worked hard to mend her as best I could. That was the end of our rabbit-raising plans. When we have a few rabbits, we house them in a much different place.

That loss was a tough one.

 BUD DeYOUNG

A REVEALING SCENT

Carrie and I raised fourteen fawns one year. Bottle-feeding those fawns was one of the biggest chores. After feeding them, we had to wipe their bottoms to keep them clean. And the fawns had to be fed at the same time or else they would fight and head butt to try to get a bottle. We hung on to bottles in each hand, between our thighs, and under our arms with those fawns knocking us over and covering us in milk. We did that three times a day for three months. It was exhausting.

These weren't the only native wildlife we took in. We raised whole litters of squirrels, chipmunks, possums, raccoons, and skunks. Most were orphans, often found beside the road with their mothers dead. People would pick them up and bring them to us.

I was pretty finished with skunks. Baby skunks have less control and are more potent than adult skunks. We can't rehabilitate skunks now with new state regulations that are trying to prevent the spread of rabies. But at that time, we took in everything until I told Carrie, "No more skunks!"

Little did I know, someone would come by with four orphaned baby skunks, and of course, Carrie wouldn't turn them away. Instead of telling me, she tucked them in the bathroom of our house.

Later in the day, one of the helpers went into the bathroom and frightened the little skunks. All four of them let loose, spraying their scent to protect themselves.

About that time, I walked into the house and was blasted by the putrid odor. "Carrie," I shouted, knowing she'd done exactly what I'd asked her not to do.

Carrie ran inside and opened all the windows. It didn't help a bit. We ended up scrubbing the bathroom and spraying every kind of deodorizer and fragrance spray throughout the house. Still, we could smell that horrendous scent everywhere.

I was not happy with Carrie over that. But it doesn't change. If I tell her she can't have something, then she goes out and gets two or more. If I don't tell her no, she might get just one.

I should learn my lesson, but the pig currently living in my bathroom proves that she does what she wants. Through this, I have come to understand that Carrie truly is as passionate about animals as I am. It can be quite annoying.

PEARL THE MISCHIEVOUS ALBINO RACCOON

The zoo hosts many visitors from big cities, people who get excited when they're driving down the road and spot a wild animal. We wanted to offer people the chance to get a good look at wildlife native to the United States and Canada and learn about their unique qualities.

So one of the projects Carrie and I implemented in the zoo expansion was a North American Trail exhibit. We built the trail and habitats and started obtaining animals, such as foxes and badgers, from other zoos.

One of the very first of these animals was an albino raccoon.

Carrie was still working in Green Bay at that time. At the school, she was known as the teacher who lived at the zoo. One day after work, she ran to another zoo to pick up a raccoon before hurrying back to the school for a mandatory meeting. Afterward, she would bring the raccoon home.

Carrie made it back in time for the meeting and snuggled that little albino raccoon into her sweatshirt. On the drive, she'd named her Pearl. Toward the end of the meeting, Carrie's belly started moving, then a little nose popped out. It caused quite the stir of excitement with the other faculty. Everybody thought Pearl was a possum because of her unique look. Pearl was small and sweet and stole all their hearts.

Pearl was raised in the house for quite a while. Being albino, she was light sensitive and immune sensitive, so she needed extra pampering. She'd go outside at certain times of the day and remain in the house the rest of the time. She was one of those characters that always kept Carrie and me entertained. She even loved the dogs and would play with them.

One day after working on a project outside, Carrie and I came in to make dinner when we stepped into a lake covering the kitchen floor. The faucet was still running, and everything appeared out of order.

Pearl had gotten out of her cage. With her tiny dexterous hands, she had opened the cupboard and refrigerator doors, and she had climbed into the sink where dishes had been soaking. Raccoons love to play in water, and somehow Pearl had turned on the faucet.

I was not happy, but Carrie just laughed and scooped up her little darling Pearl as if she'd done something wonderful.

When it was all said and done and clean again, I found the humor in it as well. But I developed a different locking system to keep Pearl from causing any more mischief.

Pearl eventually was moved to the North American Trail, where she lived out her years among other native animals and her mischievous nature caused no damage.

Cow with Ladder on His Head

Last summer as I was driving into town for supplies, a rancher from down the road waved me over. I pulled to the side of the road and waited till he reached me.

He said he was on his way to my place. "Got a heifer that stuck her head in a ladder."

I had to laugh. Animals are always full of surprises.

The rancher asked if I could tranquilize the cow so we could pull the ladder off.

I agreed. My neighbors and I help one another out; that's just what we do. It didn't matter that it was Labor Day and I had little help at the zoo because everyone

wanted the day off. The end of summer is always the last of the busiest days of the year at the zoo.

I ran home and picked up my tranq gun, then raced out to the ranch. Sure enough, there was the Black Angus with her head stuck in the ladder, and she wasn't happy about it, either. Her thrashing around in a panic proved dangerous to anyone who came close and also to herself with the weight of that ladder bending her neck and head down.

I shot her with a 2cc dart and waited, but it didn't seem to faze her. I darted her again and thought I'd give it a try. I needed to get back to the zoo right away. It was already Baby Time under the tent and close to 11:00 a.m. when we had Grizzly Feeding. The visitors would be gathering at the habitat.

Coming up beside the cow, I tried to get her free. She had turned her head to get it inside the ladder. All I needed to do was turn her or the ladder so she could get her head out. Before I could do much, the heifer moved like lightning and double-barrel kicked me. I flew back as if I'd been hit by a truck. I've never been hit so hard by anything. I was pissed.

After I got my legs back under me, I tied that cow off and yanked the ladder over her head.

Then I had to return to the zoo. The bear show started in three minutes, and it didn't happen without me.

As I flew down the country highway, the anger wore off and the pain began. It hurt just to take a breath. I've been injured enough times to know that the cow had bruised or cracked a few ribs. My back was already aching, which didn't bode well for how I'd feel the next day.

We had close to a thousand people visit the zoo that day, with a small staff of volunteers helping to man the animal encounters, do feedings, and work at the front booth. But all the shows went well. Despite my being a few minutes late, we had a really big bear show that morning. I showed my grizzly habitat, which I'm in the middle of putting in.

By evening, I was ready to collapse. We were all exhausted after that busy day. Even Louie fell asleep in one girl's arms at five o'clock.

But it took a week before the pain stopped reminding me of that cow with the ladder on her head.

 BUD DeYOUNG

CHAPTER FIFTEEN
Fifteen Minutes of Fame

The day after Christmas brings some visitors to the zoo. Not many people come up during the winter. With much of Carrie's energy going to Piper's Rescue Ranch, we're stretched thin so we don't pursue having more winter events.

But these people called asking to visit after seeing us on TV, and we always do our best to accommodate such requests. One couple was from Kenya.

Since our television show on Nat Geo WILD, we receive letters and visitors from around the world. It's been several years since we filmed, but the reruns and foreign distribution keep bringing us attention. Carrie and I love introducing our animals to anyone interested. We greatly enjoy people. But for many reasons, the strange phenomenon of being on television doesn't sit well with us.

During the summer, people often ask about the show.

Some visit because of it. They get excited to see Wallace the hippo or Emo our Bengal tiger or the other animals that were featured on the program. But it's always with mixed emotions that I talk about the experience.

It began in 2010 when Carrie posted a video of our Siberian tigers caring for their newborn cubs on YouTube.

Usually male tigers kill babies if they can in order to get the female back into heat. However, our Siberian tigers Cleo and Caesar have a bond that is unique, for any kind of animal. When we separated them during earlier births, they became so distressed being apart that we had to bring the cubs inside and bottle-feed them so the tigers could be reunited.

After observing this unique bond between Cleo and Caesar for numerous years and through many events, we considered a different plan for this pregnancy.

This time, Cleo and Caesar were together during the birth.

When we peered into the den, Caesar was cleaning the babies alongside Cleo. It is extremely rare for a male tiger to help care for the cubs.

Carrie grabbed the video camera and got some footage and then popped it onto YouTube. As far as we knew, this was one of the first documented occurrences of a male tiger helping to care for cubs in captivity.

The YouTube video became quite popular, and apparently at that time, the cable network National Geographic had staff around the United States researching zoos for a potential new series they were going to debut on their new channel Nat Geo WILD.

After someone at National Geographic saw our YouTube video, a production company contacted the zoo asking if they could tape us as a potential choice for the show.

We said sure but didn't expect too much out of it.

The production company came to the zoo, did some audios and a five-minute segment that they presented to National Geographic to see what they thought. Apparently, the company liked it a lot.

Suddenly, we were signing contracts. That was the first big challenge. Carrie spent a lot of time researching and became very good at working with the agent, ironing things out to protect our best interests. It was a crash course in being on television, and Carrie submerged herself in it, doing everything the right way.

The show came out of nowhere, and though we knew it wouldn't change us in the least, we did have hopes of improving the zoo even further by completing Wallace's humongous house, replacing buildings and barns, and finishing other projects that were on the list but scheduled for far down the road.

Then the filmmakers arrived. They wanted to script everything and have a set production schedule with an hourly agenda and a daily plan.

We explained that this wouldn't work because our

daily schedule changes constantly. An animal issue is always coming up, and when the visitors arrive, there's always something unexpected to deal with. We assured the filmmakers that they'd get plenty of material and not to worry about schedules or scripts.

We also insisted on one major condition. We weren't going to pretend to be anything but ourselves. We wouldn't stage things. All through life, my motto has been the same: "What you see is what you get."

And that's what Nat Geo WILD got as well.

For example, Carrie and I still argue often. We yell and get frustrated with one another on a regular basis. But it doesn't bother us because we understand each other. We might get mad and disagree about where to move the fox habitat or how to care for a wounded animal, but it doesn't change what's happening between us.

So the cameras came in, and we went through our same life with the film rolling around us. We did the pilot in the winter. There was a lot of added work with the film crew around, but it went well. They also went round and round trying to nail down the title of the show. Eventually they chose *My Life Is a Zoo*.

After the pilot, Nat Geo WILD wanted more. The first regular season was filmed around our Memorial Day opening and the arrival of Wallace, our hippo.

The production team was great and treated us wonderfully. We made many friends with the producers, directors, and heads of the production company, JWM Productions, who did the filming, and we met some really interesting people. We also ate well during the filming. The company set up tables of catered food under a tent by the tiger habitat.

But it was very demanding work to create a two-week program. First we'd go through our usual wearisome day, putting on the shows, caring for the animals, meeting visitors, dealing with various incidents that would invariably come up, but all the while we were being filmed.

After about six o'clock in the evening, we would spend hours reviewing the day, recording interviews, doing voice-overs, and answering any questions they had. Often this went on until eleven o'clock or so. We were already beat before this segment of our night began, and we hoped it would be worth it.

And the show was successful. Nat Geo WILD ordered more episodes and another season, with talks about a future beyond that.

Visitors from all over the world came because they'd watched *My Life Is a Zoo*. About 98 percent were fabulous people, but it also brought out 2 percent of the jerks who want to wreck what you do in life. With the supporters came those vehemently against the show and us.

Complaints were made to Nat Geo WILD, many by fanatics. We were also pressured to join major zoo associations.

The DeYoung Family Zoo is licensed and undergoes

annual inspections. We follow the rules and go above and beyond them to care for our animals. One of the most common comments visitors make is that our animals all look healthy and happy in their environments.

However, if we want to keep our entrance fees at a reasonable rate, we can't pay the high percentages to a zoo association or meet the strict rules that would take our focus away from the animals and put it on the aesthetics of the zoo. We'd rather do more for the animals than put our time, money, and energy into paving our walkways, planting flower gardens, putting in expensive bathrooms and picnic tables, or blacktopping the parking lot.

Carrie and I live in the same small prefab house that was set up in one day back in 1979. Our finances mainly go toward caring for the animals, building new habitats, and improving their lives. That's more important to us than anything else. We weren't going to change our focus on the zoo and animals because we were on a TV show.

Our detractors weren't visitors to the zoo. They were people who watched the show and made judgments.

Threats were made. Lawyers became involved.

And then the show was cancelled.

Our life was good prior to television. Everything was going well.

But after television, our donations dried right up because everybody thought we made boatloads of money

BUD DeYOUNG

for being on the show, but that was not the case. We got a first season rate, which was not much. Since the show was cancelled, we've had some hard years.

Being on TV never went to my head or Carrie's. We are always humbled when someone wants our autograph. There's a sense of awkwardness to it that just doesn't fit with us. I don't have two socks that match, and I didn't on the show, either.

But people looked at us differently. I didn't change—didn't change clothes from what I wore prior to that, still took no vacations, and so forth. Life just went on. We went on TV, and we went off TV. They prepare you for being on TV, but they don't prepare you for not being on it, such as how you'll deal with people assuming things about you or treating you differently.

When it was all said and done, most of the money we received from the show was spent on attorney fees. Months of stress and dealing with the fallout took away most of the enjoyment of having the show.

The only good that really came out has been the people we've met and the letters we've received from all over the world. That has been really touching.

I guess some ideas fail when you live your dream. It's never a smooth, easy path. Anyone who thinks that's what it's like to reach your dream is fooling himself.

It's hard work. It's stress. It has moments of failure.

But even in the midst of all that, I still feel a deep sense of satisfaction that I'm right where I'm supposed to be.

A young Wallace discovers his new habitat and takes a bite of some fresh carrots. This was a big step for the zoo!

CHAPTER SIXTEEN
An African Hippo in the Upper Peninsula

"Are you interested in a baby bull hippo?"

The question came from a zoo in Indonesia. Carrie spends a lot of time talking with zoos around the world as she studies and searches for unique animals to bring to the DeYoung Family Zoo.

Zoos usually don't keep bull calf hippos because when they grow they'll kill the other calves that are born there. So this zoo in Jakarta was seeking a new home for their newborn.

Carrie has a soft spot for hippos. When she taught preschool, the kids loved singing the hippo song and hearing Carrie talk about them. One student even gave her a stuffed hippo as a gift, and every year they asked if the zoo had gotten a hippopotamus yet.

"No way," I replied when Carrie brought up the subject.

We already had the usual variety of animals that many private zoos have, such as big cats, wolves, and bears.

Now we were adding more unusual critters, especially with Carrie's connections to zoos worldwide. We wanted to offer our visitors the opportunity to see an exotic or unique creature up close and to gain knowledge about the great diversity and amazing features of animals all over the globe.

We'd already brought some hyenas to the Upper Peninsula, and Carrie incorporated an educational element about them into the daily summer shows. She loves the hyenas and didn't like that most visitors had an adverse opinion of them. Some of that prejudice stems from the movie *The Lion King* and the hyenas' image as cowardly scavengers. Hyenas are actually very intelligent and quite good at hunting. Though they appear canine, they're more closely related to a feline.

We were happy with the addition of the hyenas and excited to obtain exotics that would set us apart and bring new educational opportunities to our visitors. Already we'd been added to the list seeking not just any chimpanzee but an orphaned chimpanzee. Around this time, we finally brought home Louie after a six-year wait.

"Maybe we should get a hippo," Carrie said, bringing up the subject again as we discussed ideas.

I thought she was crazy, but Carrie set to work researching, as she does. We discussed the requirements to accommodate not only one but eventually more hippos. Because hippos are colony-type, social animals and live in large groups, the bull calf would eventually need a female in the coming years, and females were harder to find.

Finally, a plan was created, and even though I'd been hesitant, I was thrilled.

Carrie started the paperwork, which was a major undertaking. Since hippos aren't endangered, the process was a little easier because we didn't need to work with the U.S. Department of the Interior. But the U.S. Department of Agriculture had many requirements to bring a hippo in from another country. With things like insects that could be transferred from Indonesia to the United States, we had to create a plan for disinfecting and quarantining the animal.

Then Carrie and I argued over where to put the hippo habitat. Every time we decided on one area, I thought of a reason it wouldn't work. We ended up back in the original site we'd chosen but with better reasons why. That's how Carrie and I tend to make things better. Others perceive our unusual discussions as flat-out warring arguments, but for us, that's how we get things done.

As plans moved forward, I got the site for the hippo habitat excavated. We needed two-ton building blocks called Texas roadblocks, which we poured.

We were behind schedule but finally had everything ready. The hippo's initial outdoor habitat was built with a small pool in it, perfect for a baby hippo, the paperwork was complete, and the transport plans were initiated. It was time to get the hippo.

By then, Nat Geo WILD was with us, filming the final stages and covering our hippo's arrival to Chicago from Jakarta. It was the largest project we'd ever undertaken.

After numerous snags, enormous last-minute fee increases, and time in quarantine, we finally brought the hippo to the DeYoung Family Zoo.

Wallace was a huge hit.

Wallace has certainly been the most difficult animal to maintain at the zoo. We built a larger outdoor habitat as he outgrew his first baby hippo one. It cost something like twenty thousand dollars for building blocks and excavations. Fred Reidell and his son, Travis, dug a heart-shaped pond where Wallace resides much of the summer. Then, of course, we have the winter months and the daily work keeping Wallace clean in his eighty-five-degree environment. We take about a thousand pounds of manure from there every week. I swear, the food goes straight through him, and he's still gaining weight. He's three thousand pounds already.

We're seeking a mate for our hippo and have a few options in Colombia and Brazil.

There's also the huge half-finished building that will house numerous hippos. Hopefully, we'll get it built soon. It's attached to Wallace's outdoor habitat and separated by a gate. When spring comes, we'll just open the gate and he'll go out. The money issue keeps us from progressing with a few of these plans.

These are some of the challenges of having an African hippopotamus in Michigan's Upper Peninsula. Yet I can't imagine the zoo without Wallace now. He has quite the personality, and he's become our biggest attraction. People from all over the country and the world come to our little corner to see him. They get an up close look at this amazing creature. They get to see his enormous size and the inside of his mouth when I feed him and hear about a hippo's habits and personality. Some visitors get to pop a whole head of romaine into his mouth and feel his breath on their faces.

I think back to that night when Carrie said, "We should get a hippo."

We did it. A hippo at our zoo! It was almost more than I'd dreamed.

A very young Louie gets his checkup after taking a bath. The health and safety of our critters is extremely important to us.

CHAPTER SEVENTEEN
Real Structure for Real Dreams

Zoos are required to have a veterinarian.

Every zoo in the country must have a Class C license with the U.S. Department of Agriculture, which is especially for exhibiting animals. All zoos are under the same jurisdiction, governing board, and regulations.

Beyond the license, there are different organizations available but not required, such as the Association of Zoos and Aquariums (AZA) and the Zoological Association of America (ZAA). These organizations require their own standards for care, quality, control, and exhibition on top of the USDA requirements. We are members of the ZAA. Our goal is to continue moving forward as the zoo without giving up our core values of keeping our animals' best interests first and foremost.

One prerequisite for a Class C license is the availability of a veterinarian around the clock. Our wonderful vet, Colleen Heitman, has a private practice where she sees large mammals and the usual barnyard animals. She probably never expected to care for so many exotic animals.

I can't remember exactly how I approached Colleen twenty-odd years ago. Most likely it was out of need when I took various animals to the vet clinic. Then she started coming on-site when an animal needed surgery or neutering.

Various issues arise with our animals that are beyond our experience. That's when Colleen steps in.

Over the years, she's done a variety of surgeries, assisted in births, and helped Carrie with the sick, injured, and abused domestic animals that come to the rescue ranch. Colleen amputated the leg of a female wolf that tried to overthrow the alpha female and was terribly injured in the fight. She's also patched up goats with broken legs that were on the losing end of head-butting matches. We have a well-rounded vet.

In the past few years, one practice we implemented at the zoo is neutering the majority of our tigers. There are many tigers in captivity and they breed well, but not many facilities can handle large carnivores. We won't allow any of our cats into private ownership to be raised as pets. I don't believe in that. So instead of creating an excess of tigers, we have them neutered.

Colleen does the neutering and spaying at the zoo. During the third episode of the Nat Geo WILD show, we had our white tiger Emo neutered. Emo came from Florida a number of years ago. He was a rescue cat with very poor genetics. He has abnormalities like crossed eyes and male malformations, which are a result of inbreeding. The facility he came from was popping out white tigers left and right because they could be sold legally and there's a demand for white tiger cubs.

Our white tiger, Emo. Education is key for a better and brighter future for these magnificent animals!

We get a lot of questions about Emo from visitors. Many places would hide away an imperfect animal or get rid of him, but every creature is special and loved at the DeYoung Family Zoo. We don't hide him away. We can answer the questions, and Emo can be enjoyed for himself.

However, we had Emo neutered so he wouldn't pass on his genes.

These are the kinds of decisions we make often with advice from Colleen.

Our license requires our vet to do four inspection visits annually. However, Colleen does more than four, frequently coming out monthly. While we do the preventative work, such as inoculations and maintenance on the animals, we appreciate having Colleen regularly inspect the animals in case there's something we might not spot.

The daily work is certainly on my shoulders and Carrie's. But with people like Colleen as well as Dereck, Bart, Hayden, our summer volunteers, the locals, and regional people who've helped with everything from bottle-feeding babies to excavating ponds, the DeYoung Family Zoo operates through the summer and has grown into what it is today. We couldn't have done it without them, and we continue to thrive because of community support, amazing volunteers, and, of course, our own love of the animals.

CHAPTER EIGHTEEN
The Strength of a Backbone

I am going through old pictures and papers tonight, and the memories get stacked one upon the other. Carrie is still at the rescue. She won't be home until late. She and Linda, the vet for the rescue, are at the birthing of one of Carrie's horses.

The photographs, letters, cards, and certificates bring up memories and the knowledge of what I can forget while performing the day-to-day chores and meeting other needs.

But tonight I pause and reflect and feel proud of what's been built here. And I remember a saying, "The person who thinks he knows everything is the dumbest person there is."

I've made this remark before, and this won't be the last time.

My mom gave me backbone in pursuing my dreams. She encouraged me to do what would make me happy. She did this with gentle pushes and a few hard kicks now and again. I'll always feel indebted to her.

I'm very good at a lot of things. But there's one area of my life that I struggled with some: insecurity. I've had plenty of failures and made many mistakes, but I'm tough as nails, can work circles around kids forty years younger than me, and I've had to solve all kinds of complex problems. But I don't have a college education.

Many people in the zoo business expect other people in the zoo business to have traveled the same educational step-by-step path that they traveled. They don't respect a different way.

Carrie gave me more backbone about this. I suppose it's a lot like my mom: she believes in me and offered me that belief as well.

Carrie gave me a backbone to stand up to people who make false remarks or disrespect me.

People sometimes question how I can run a zoo without a college education. First of all, I couldn't go to college right out of high school. After my dad passed away, I worked and helped my mom while I lived at home. Then I married Penny and moved to Michigan to work on a farm and in the woods. I couldn't go to college then.

And the truth is, I wasn't much into schooling. I have always learned by doing. Too many kids are forced to attend college or else are treated as if they can't amount to anything.

I've always been hungry to learn all sorts of things. And I put my full energy into it. I read everything about my interests and asked questions. I talked to experts and studied and implemented their advice.

That's why I'll say it again: "The person who thinks he knows everything is the dumbest person there is."

We can learn something from every person we encounter.

People in the Upper Peninsula work hard for their living and are often some of the smartest people out there. And there aren't university classes that teach the kinds of skills people need to thrive in such regions.

The people who think they're full of knowledge and stop listening to others stop learning and hearing. Those are the most ignorant people in the world.

I'm no longer self-conscious about my lack of a college education. We do a great job with our animals here. Visitors comment continually about the health and contentment of our critters. Our federal zoo inspector gives us praise as well. The governor of Michigan presented me with a certificate of special recognition saying that we are doing great work for the economy and for education. These are proud moments, and they confirm that we're on track.

Sure, attending college is important. It's the way most people should go, and I'd recommend it to most any kid who asked me. But college isn't for everyone. Nothing is for everyone. Education can come from college, books, blisters on your hands, spending time in the environment you're interested in, reading, and just getting out and doing things. It comes from opening your ears and never thinking you've learned enough.

And I'm not the first man without a college degree to build something from a dream. Sometimes it helps to remember some of them: Richard Branson, international business owner. Daniel Boone, frontiersman and explorer. Walt Disney, creator of the Magic Kingdom. Peter Jennings, television news anchor. Jack London, author and journalist (and lover of wolves). Charles Lindbergh, aviator, author, inventor, and explorer. Claude Monet, impressionist painter. Ansel Adams, photographer and environmentalist. George Eastman, inventor and founder of Kodak. Charles Culpeper, owner and CEO of Coca-Cola. Steve Jobs, cofounder of Apple.

I wonder if these people experienced flak because of their lack of a college education. Yet they were prepared to pursue their dreams regardless, and so am I.

CHAPTER NINETEEN
Letting Go

Tomorrow is the last day of the year, and we're watching Louie wreak havoc through the house. He tries to get into my cookie jar, then grabs the dish drainer and tosses it, unrolls paper towels, and acts like he's sweeping the floor. He watches Carrie and me doing chores and mimics what we do. Louie's outgrowing the house, which means he's outgrowing us.

I can't count how many bears, lions, tigers, wolves, warthogs, kangaroos, porcupines, skunks, raccoons, spider monkeys, snow monkeys, and baboons we've raised in this house over the years.

When I look around the place, the memories come to life. I see the day when the kids were still here and I came home and found the house looking like a federal disaster area. Inside the kennel, the baboon was sitting with the blanket on top of his head. The latch to his cage was undone.

Apparently, the kids had brought the baboon out to show their friends, then forgot to latch the cage. When the house was empty, the mischievous guy got out and had his fun. And that baboon knew he'd done wrong and was hiding his head when I got there.

With animals, there's never a boring moment. And I don't think I will ever live in a house where there are no animals.

Soon Louie will not be living in our home, not only because the house will not hold him even with his own room, play gym, outside yard, and toys but because chimps need to be with other chimps. They need to become the animals they are, not forced into a human environment. He is still an infant right now, just two and a half years old, but I don't think he'll be able to stay in the house next year. So this summer, one major project will be erecting a heated primate building for Louie.

Carrie and I bring all these animals into our home, into our daily lives, and most of all, into our hearts. We have to change our routine and arrangement of the house to hand raise babies of different species and those with diverse needs. We sacrifice sleep and space and privacy.

We fall in love with them. Then we have to let them go.

It's one of the challenges of caring for critters: saying good-bye even if it's just moving them into their habitats.

We know the relationship changes with that step, as it must. This is part of being responsible to the animal, even while it breaks our hearts in the process.

It's a feeling I've become all too familiar with over time.

Bud and Carrie discussing future plans for the zoo and their next big enclosure plans for the bears and wolves.

CHAPTER TWENTY
Regrets and Moving On

After Penny and I divorced, my father-in-law Dutch wouldn't talk to me for years. Even after Penny remarried and moved on with her life, he would have nothing to do with me.

Perhaps he still thought of me as a bit crazy from that time I took him out in my Corvette and again when I brought a bear cub to live in the house. Penny and I tried keeping Honeybear a secret from Dutch. Eventually, he found out. A little bear cub couldn't remain a secret for long.

"You have a bear living in your house?" he'd said incredulously. For such a practical and penny-pinching person, Dutch couldn't understand why anyone would have a hungry, growing bear join the family with no use or purpose there.

But despite our differences, Dutch and I had worked wearisome hours side by side in the woods and around our places and endured adverse weather conditions—and all this for more than two decades. Dutch and I were more than just good buddies. We were like father and son.

I kept my distance, hoping he'd come around. I missed Dutch and my mother-in-law Juanita after so many years of being close. Their farm wasn't far away, but Dutch had made it clear he didn't want to see me.

After Juanita passed away, I regretted not having done more to mend the fences. She had been a wonderful woman. Kind, hardworking, always ready to help us out. I missed her, and I hoped she knew how much she'd meant to me.

Finally, I'd had enough. *Screw it,* I thought and headed over to the Truitt farm, where I'd first visited in my teenage years with George Dragic.

I wasn't sure how Dutch would greet me. It might have been with his shotgun.

He surprised me by welcoming me inside his home.

At last, we talked. And after that, I visited Dutch or he stopped by the zoo, and we came to a good place, enjoying our time talking and reminiscing.

Dutch died about three years after we made amends. Swallowing my pride and having those last years together are things I'm grateful for.

I don't spend much time rehashing my life and allowing regrets to slow me down. Life moves forward: we have fund-raisers for Piper's Rescue Ranch, the grizzly habitat needs new poles in the fence line, the daily chores must get done, and I draw up plans for the future habitats and zoo expansion. But there are certainly a few things I'd redo if I could.

I missed Grandma Ruth's funeral because I couldn't take time off from work. I regret that and should have quit what I was doing and gone down there. Grandma Ruth was an inspiration to me as I was growing up. She helped Mom and us kids when my dad passed away. She was one tough woman, an awesome cook, and very encouraging.

I also wish I'd taken my kids on vacations and done more activities like that. We once went to Walt Disney World, but during most of their growing-up years I was working and raising animals. Now my children have families of their own.

Carry is a registered nurse and worked for a long time in the ER. Right now, she's furthering her education.

Bradley became an RN as well. He works in a catheterization laboratory, helping to save lives every day.

Becky still works with animals. She's a herdswoman for a large dairy farm and also has her own horses and other animals.

I'm proud of each one of my children. They are great people, and they're raising wonderful children of their own. I'm blessed with amazing grandchildren: Wyatt, Darrien, Jacob, Damion, Bailey, and Jenna.

If only we could tell our younger selves exactly what to do. But life doesn't work that way. I can't imagine there's one man on earth who doesn't look back and wish to change portions of his life.

There's always a price to live your dream. That price is different for every person. For me it includes the struggles of winter, losing front teeth, uncommon house repairs, letting animals be animals when I might want to keep them close, having regrets I can't rectify, and giving my entire life with no vacations, no sick days, and no escapes from this one thing.

That's the price I pay. For all the good and the bad, it's the path I've taken and the one I'm supposed to be on.

BUD DeYOUNG

PART THREE

The Purpose

CHAPTER TWENTY-ONE

Hope in the Air

Spring is coming.

You wouldn't know it from the frozen world we remain trapped in. I'm still numb with cold throughout the day, but we've reached the hump and are making our way toward the days we at the zoo love the best. We're like kids waiting to go to Disney World. Tucked between the immediate needs of firewood, keeping animals safe during blizzards, picking up beef and butchering it for the tigers, the anticipation grows. I imagine releasing the animals into sunshine, start checklists of projects we hope to accomplish this year, and picture the people filling the grounds, excited to see the animals.

We set our opening date. *April 1, April 1, April 1* repeats in our heads like a mantra. Springtime is still hidden deep down, but it's beginning to tap at the hardened shell of winter. It grows stronger even as storms continue to blast us.

I guess in a way, spring is like passion reborn after the

hardships that invariably come our way.

Bit by bit over many years, I built this zoo. There have been challenges every step of the way but many springtime moments throughout the journey. In the past ten years, the zoo has known fast expansion, and it's still developing.

As a child, I stayed up late many nights, working on plans for my zoo, sketching houses and habitats for animals. I still stay up late working on plans for the primate house, the new section for the wolves, with dreams for even more. The dreaming never stops.

But along the way, a surprising thing happened beyond my own plans. I think this is the nature of a passion. Pursuing dreams opens up visions beyond what a person initially wanted. That's certainly happened many times over for me.

The dreams take on a life of their own and work their way beyond one or two individuals; they leap over us and touch lives in ways we could never imagine.

These stories surprise me, and I'm in complete awe at how dreams continue to grow far beyond my sight.

BUD DeYOUNG

CHAPTER TWENTY-TWO
The Wolf Test

After Penny and I divorced and I was dating for many years, one way I'd get to know a woman was by introducing her to the wolves. The wolves have a way of

understanding people, as not even humans can perceive.

On that first day Carrie volunteered at the zoo, I had a lot of running around to do, so I asked her to stay at the house and tend to a little monkey named Fred. Fred was a Japanese macaque and quite a handful. I was gone for hours and wondered how Carrie had fared with the little

Wolves are extremely intelligent animals and travel in packs. They don't easily accept new members into their packs, but thankfully Carrie was one of those honored few who were.

BUD DeYOUNG

fella. I couldn't believe it when I returned and Fred was still out and actually behaving quite well. Carrie had even taught him a few things.

I was definitely attracted to Carrie. After my visitors left, I took her on a tour of the zoo. We rode the four-wheeler around, stopping to talk about different animals. Then I brought her to the wolf pen.

Carrie was fond of dogs; I knew that already. But wolves are more intelligent canines. They can be crafty with their allegiance to the pack, whereas a dog is usually more about loyalty to his or her master. Well, I took Carrie inside the wolf habitat. We sat down side by side on a large log and didn't talk. It was peaceful as the sound of the woods folded in around us.

Soon the wolves came. They moved closer and closer, surrounding us. Within moments, they took to Carrie, rubbing on her, licking her face, and trying to sit in her lap. She laughed while stroking their hair as they pushed against one another to get near her.

I just watched, grinning. We were there for a long time with Carrie completely wrapped up with the wolves and my wolves completely wrapped up with her.

Finally, she seemed to realize the time. Carrie had to drive back to Green Bay that night. We said good-bye to the wolves and walked back to the house. She thanked me for the amazing experience.

I couldn't wipe that smile off my face. I finally admitted

that my number one test was to take someone into the wolf pen. "If the wolves like you, then you're for sure a good person." And the wolves had loved her. "I hope to see you again."

It was incredible how comfortable I felt with Carrie. There was no uneasiness, and it felt as if we'd known each other our entire lives. Of course, she was much younger than I was, but the age difference disappeared as well. I hugged her good-bye, then watched her walk to the parking lot.

I went inside and raced around, searching for a pen and paper.

She hadn't left yet. As I approached her truck, I saw her just sitting there, deep in thought. I knocked on the window, then gave her my number and asked for hers. I couldn't bear her driving off and leaving me to wonder all week if she'd be back. I wanted to talk to her more right now, but I knew she had to leave.

We talked every day that week. She returned the following weekend and the weekend after that. Then eventually, I wouldn't let her go.

CHAPTER TWENTY-THREE
Wolf Pack

After Carrie's first encounter with the wolves, she was drawn to them in a very deep way. She dived into learning everything she could about them.

She also spent tons of time with the animals, learning directly from them as well as what she read and gained from experts. In no time, the wolves accepted Carrie as a member of the pack.

Before long, if any wolf-related problems came up, Carrie was the go-to person. She worked with the animals or addressed the issue, and I enjoyed watching her take the lead.

We didn't have many wolves at this time. Some of my first ones had passed away, and I was building up other areas of the zoo. But Carrie and I discussed building our wolf packs and dreamed of getting a black British Columbian wolf like the one I'd had in the past. However, this particular coloring and breed was expensive and difficult to find.

There are many people who become special friends of ours and of the animals at the zoo. Berna McQueen, or Sissy, as everyone called her, was one of those people. She was an amazing, beautiful older lady with a lot of spunk.

Sissy had been coming to the zoo for some time, and when she and Carrie met the first summer that Carrie lived here, the two connected right away.

Sissy had a special love for the wolves as well. When the park was quiet after hours, Carrie took Sissy into the wolf pack with her. Our friend was thrilled at the chance to be with the wolves, and the animals took to her immediately. After that, Sissy became a vocal advocate for us getting more wolves. But we didn't have the funds, so the two women tried to take matters into their own hands and started a fund-raiser to purchase a wolf. It didn't get very far.

In the Upper Peninsula and most northern states, the existence of wolves is a controversial subject. Many of the farmers and ranchers would rather the animals have remained extinct in the United States because of the losses to their livestock. The reintroduction of wolves has been contentious, with widely varying opinions and studies. So raising funds for a wolf, even though it was for our zoo and some people love them, was a pretty tough goal.

When the fund-raiser ended, Sissy donated the money to buy a wolf pup.

Soon afterward, Carrie and I found a litter of black

British Columbian pups in Illinois. We were so excited. After we finished our chores one afternoon, we left a helper at the zoo, and off we went to pick up a wolf pup.

We arrived at the park very late at night, and the owners led us outside with flashlights to see the pups. Carrie was given the honor of choosing, and she picked a handsome little male just like we had hoped to find.

During our search for a new wolf, another park asked if we'd pick up a female timber wolf at this same zoo and drop her off to them on our way home. This litter of pups was a little older and in a different area.

Carrie went to view them with one of the park owners.

She entered the pen and observed the pups. There was one female that had something unique about her. This small wolf came up to Carrie immediately, studied her, then turned and looked at the other pups that remained huddled together. The pup moved closer to Carrie, smelled her, and then walked away. It was as if she gave her approval, because as she left Carrie, the other pups raced up to Carrie, climbing all over her lap. The unique pup stood off to the side, studying the scene.

Carrie felt a strong connection to the female wolf. But Carrie kept her back to the wolf until the animal crept up closer and closer, smelled her a few times, and then nudged her head under Carrie's arm. Carrie looked down at that little face staring up at her.

"This is the one," Carrie said. The wolf's intelligence, courage, and the fact that she was obviously in charge weighed greatly in the decision, not to mention that the wolf liked Carrie.

"Are you sure?" the park owner asked. She explained that the wolf was odd, not like the others. They hadn't been sure what to do with her.

This only confirmed the decision for Carrie.

Now that we had the wolves, Carrie and I headed straight back to upper Michigan. Our black pup sat on Carrie's lap as I drove, and the female curled up on her feet, where she stayed the entire trip. Off and on, that little wolf looked up at Carrie as if to see that everything was going well, then she'd curl up again. If she wanted attention, she'd nudge Carrie's foot, then look away, pretending she hadn't done anything. Carrie would pet her when she did this. We also saw how she watched our black male wolf to be sure he wasn't making trouble.

"Can't we keep her too? She's so smart. Can't we find a way?" Carrie begged as we drove.

But we didn't have the money, and we had promised the other park that we would deliver their female timber wolf.

Carrie had a tough time handing over the female pup, and it broke my heart to watch the scene as we said good-bye.

Once back on the road, we turned the focus to our black British Columbian wolf. He was a sweet little guy, and he needed a name. Since Sissy Berna McQueen had donated the funds, we named him Berna after her.

We couldn't wait for Sissy to meet him. We knew she would be as eager as we were to have a new wolf at our zoo. We expected her immediately after we called to tell her of the wolf's arrival, but the days stretched into weeks and then into months with no visit from Sissy.

Finally at the end of summer, Sissy arrived at the zoo. She was still her high-spirited and outgoing self, but something was definitely wrong.

Sissy played with Berna, who had grown considerably in the months since we'd brought him home. She took a lot of photos and stayed until the park closed. I left to give Sissy and Carrie time together with the wolves.

After Sissy went home, Carrie cried as she told me what happened. Sissy had walked to a downed log and sat down with a somberness coming over her. All the wolves immediately went to her, acting solemn as well, as if they sensed what was going on. Then Sissy told Carrie that she had cancer.

We tried to stay in contact with Sissy as Berna grew up. Then one day, Sissy visited, and it was clear that our friend didn't have long to live. The wolves raced to her, licking and rubbing on her. It was amazing to see how they reacted to her.

We set up a chair in with the wolves, since it was hard for Sissy to get up and down, and gave her time alone with the animals she loved so much. The wolves sat by her, resting quietly. Berna sat with her for a long time.

Sissy died a short time later.

The next spring, Berna fathered his first litter, but only one female pup survived. We named her Sissy. But Sissy the pup was runty with an abnormally large head.

Carrie pulled her from the wolf habitat and bottle-fed her after the other pups died and the vet gave a bad report about little Sissy's future. The wolf probably had water on the brain and, if she survived, would be prone to seizures. More than likely, the pup was going to die.

Carrie always champions the underdog, and I watched

BUD DeYOUNG

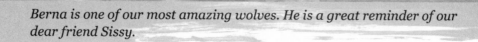

Berna is one of our most amazing wolves. He is a great reminder of our dear friend Sissy.

her nurture the wolf pup with great devotion and energy. Sissy looked so odd with her small body and large head, but she was a fighter like the woman she was named for. And even with our friend Sissy gone, it seemed her spirit reached out and gave that little pup a fighting chance.

Eventually, our wolf Sissy grew into her head and became a beautiful wolf. Even the vet couldn't believe it. Sissy was still smaller than the other wolves, so she always looked like an older pup instead of a full-grown wolf, but she didn't act like it.

We contacted the family of our dear friend Sissy and told them the story of our wolf pup and what we'd named her. They replied with a photograph of our friend and a letter telling the story of Sissy as a child that made both Carrie and me break down in tears.

Apparently, Sissy had complications and numerous health issues when she was young. These only made her stronger, and she became the outgoing woman everyone adored, so full of compassion, humor, and love.

Sissy the wolf later had two gorgeous puppies, a female and a male, both with black coloring. Those puppies out-grew their mom to the point that people thought Sissy was the puppy and the babies were the parents. But Sissy is still a beautiful wolf, and she'll always hold a special place in our hearts.

It's times like this when the animal and the human worlds connect in ways beyond what we can envision. Maybe it was coincidence that this wolf named Sissy had so many attributes like the woman Sissy, or perhaps our friend's spirit was there through the fight to save the little pup, but I've spent enough years with animals to know that there are connections we cannot understand or explain. They are indescribably real, so I just recognize them, hold them close, and am awed and inspired when they occur.

CHAPTER TWENTY-FOUR
The Three-Legged Wolf

A couple of years after we brought home Berna the wolf and dropped off the little unique timber wolf that Carrie had become so attached to, we received a call from the park where we'd left her.

For a while, that zoo put a lot of time into their wolves, building habitats for them and asking us for advice. I shared my experiences, and Carrie and I took our crew down there to build them a wolf habitat just like ours. They had some older wolves and Rio, the female pup we'd dropped off to them.

But the older wolves passed away, and they had only the one unique wolf left. Instead of adding more wolves, they decided to use the habitat for other animals. They asked if we wanted their timber wolf.

There was no need to discuss it. Fate was bringing Carrie and that wolf back together, and we couldn't wait to go pick her up.

Whenever we bring in a new animal, it needs to be quarantined and then we find the right way to blend it with the other animals, especially when you're dealing with pack animals like wolves.

We had to ease Rio into the pack by first blending her with the younger pups. After they were integrated, we brought Rio and the pups in with the other wolves in the big habitat. Then the younger wolves, older wolves, and Rio were able to run in one large pack. This took months, and Carrie did most of the work. She spent time with the wolves to help them become comfortable until they behaved like one family.

Rio took right to the pack, and they took to her. The younger wolves followed her around as if she were their mother and pack leader. For the entire summer and autumn months, the pack ran together.

Then breeding season arrived. During breeding season, the fight for dominance can cause issues. Each pack has one alpha female and one alpha male. Only the alphas are allowed to mate and have pups. The alphas are the first to eat, they are the bosses, and they are the parents. The rest of the wolves must remain in their places below the alpha. If a female other than the alpha becomes pregnant during breeding season, the other wolves will kill her newborn pups. This is how a pack survives in the wild. If there were too many pups, the burden to feed and protect them might jeopardize the entire pack.

BUD DeYOUNG

Rio displayed alpha characteristics since that first moment Carrie saw her as a young wolf. She was brave and daring, and with breeding season upon her, Rio decided to challenge the alpha female for dominance.

Rio was young, maybe only two or three. The established alpha female, Whisper, had been alpha for a long time. Whisper was a strong and sassy wolf. So one day at the peak of breeding season, Rio decided to make her move. Neither Carrie nor I saw it coming since Rio had behaved submissively during her integration into the pack. She had probably been plotting this move the entire time.

The fight was horrendous.

We heard the sounds and chaos across the zoo. Carrie was running inside the wolf habitat by the time I arrived. She'd bonded with the wolves to the point that she was even more of an alpha than Whisper, and when Carrie was inside the enclosure, Whisper returned to omega status.

I yelled at Carrie to get out of there, but she was already diving in to break up the fight. It was a nasty battle of wolves yelping and snarling with hair and blood flying. Carrie pulled the two wolves apart and grabbed Rio, screaming for me and the boys to get the bike.

We drove Rio up to the house and were stunned by her injuries. Rio sat there, brave and calm, looking at us as if she believed we would help her. But among her many injuries, her front leg was destroyed. The skin and muscle had separated completely from the bone.

Carrie burst into tears. "We've got to save her," she bawled.

I tried to comfort her, but the truth was there before our eyes. This wolf wasn't going to make it.

Carrie shouted that Rio was tough, she was a fighter, and she could survive on three legs. I tried to reason with her, but she wouldn't listen. We wrapped up the wolf and raced to the vet clinic.

The vet confirmed what I had said, but Carrie wouldn't have any of it. If Rio were a dog, then losing a leg wouldn't be a tragedy. But a wolf needs its pack, and no pack was going to accept a three-legged member into its family. They'd kill her for sure.

Carrie insisted that she would make it work, but first we needed to save Rio's life.

Our amazing vet took over. She was forced to amputate Rio's leg up to her shoulder. She allowed Carrie to stay in for the surgery.

We brought Rio home wrapped up and sitting on Carrie's lap. It reminded me of the day we'd driven home from Illinois with this same wolf curled up at Carrie's feet.

Carrie can imitate the howl of the wolves and get them howling with her. But when we brought Rio home, only two days after we'd raced off with her to the vet, we stepped out of the truck in the parking lot far beyond the wolf habitat, and those wolves immediately sounded off without any provocation. It was as if they could sense or smell that Rio was back. All across the zoo, the sound of their howling echoed as we carried Rio into the house.

And then the work really began.

Learning to walk and get around without a front leg would be a tough transition. Beyond the physical healing, there was also the matter of the pack. Without a strong spirit, Rio would have never made it. But since the moment we first saw her at that Illinois park when she'd studied Carrie so intently, we knew she was a different wolf.

The day we brought Rio home from the vet, Carrie rubbed her gently all over and then went immediately to the wolf habitat. The wolves came up to her slowly, smelling, rubbing against her, and licking Carrie's face. Carrie felt no animosity toward the wolves. She'd been at the zoo and with the wolves long enough to understand the nature of the wild. Whisper and the other wolves didn't hate Rio; it was just their way.

The wolves began to howl again. From the house, Rio called back even while stretched out prone inside the nursery. Carrie returned with tears in her eyes to see her beloved Rio without a leg, beat to hell, and unable to get up, but calling to her pack. I knew Carrie was more resolved than ever to make this work, but I was still pretty doubtful.

Carrie worked tirelessly with Rio between each of our other animal responsibilities. At times, Carrie had to force Rio to slow down and not overdo it while she healed.

In the meantime, Carrie continued to carry the wolves'

scents back and forth between Rio and the pack. As the true alpha, she believed this would help them accept Rio when the time came.

The day soon arrived when Carrie decided Rio was rehabbed enough to return to the wolf pack.

I was worried, not just for Rio but for Carrie as well, knowing she'd be heartbroken if the pack turned on Rio. And there was also the possible danger to Carrie herself.

She scoffed at my concerns.

Carrie carried Rio into the wolf habitat, as she'd carried her out of it after the fight. She sat down with Rio in her lap. I watched at the gate, nervous and angry that Carrie wouldn't listen to a word I said. I just knew the wolves were going to tear Rio apart the first chance they got.

Carrie was convinced that she knew her pack and everything would be okay.

The first wolf to approach was Berna, the black male British Columbian we'd picked up with Rio so long ago. He licked Carrie and then lay down beside her and Rio. One by one, the other wolves came over. Their excitement grew as they began to lick and smell Rio and Carrie.

Whisper was the final wolf to approach, but at last, she came to them as well. She studied the pair, then licked Carrie and then Rio. And with that, Rio was accepted back into the pack.

I must admit that I was shocked. And my surprise didn't end there. Rio defied the odds as she grew stronger and became a vital part of the pack, with only three legs. She learned to run and keep up with the other wolves. And Rio is so crafty that she took sticks in her mouth and placed them in the openings to help her get in and out as she dug a complex system of wolf dens with only one front leg.

Years later, Rio even gained alpha female position twice and gave birth to two litters of puppies.

Some very content wolves just relaxing the day away.

Carrie and I butt heads on just about everything. We also have to consider the reputation of the zoo, which we do in different ways. When people question and spread rumors about the health of our animals or our practices because they see a three-legged wolf or a starving animal we've recently rescued, I want to be mindful of these animals on exhibition.

Carrie believes in showing every animal to the public—healthy, whole, or not. We argue about such subjects, but the letters accusing us of harming our animals are harder for me to take than they are for her. But with Rio? I can't deny the miracle Carrie worked with those wolves.

During the summer, Carrie tells our visitors the story of Rio the three-legged wolf. She uses it to illustrate how amazing animals and humans can be even if they aren't what we'd consider a perfect specimen.

Such reminders push us beyond what is normal to see the beauty and qualities in a unique world where nothing is truly normal.

BUD DeYOUNG

CHAPTER TWENTY-FIVE
Nala the "Pet" Lioness

In man's quest to connect with the animal world, sometimes people become confused about the purpose of wildlife.

Back when the film *The Lion King* was released in the early nineties, lion cubs became a popular toy for children whose parents buy these kinds of extravagant gifts. Lions could still be privately purchased without much difficulty, especially in states such as Ohio. A cub could be bought for about five hundred bucks. The problem came when the adorable cub began to grow.

My zoo had two large habitats for bears and wolves, and I'd obtained my first male lion named Kenya. I wanted to get Kenya a mate eventually, but I wasn't planning to anytime soon.

Then out of the blue, a man called from Dayton, Ohio, with an issue. He had a six-month-old lioness he wanted me to take off his hands. The man explained that he was a dentist and his wife was an attorney, and they worked long hours. Their children were six and eight years old, and they had begged to have a lion cub after seeing *The Lion King.* So they found a breeder and brought home the cub.

It wasn't long before the little lioness became more than they could handle. The man said if I'd come and take Nala, it would be a great favor to him. I was more than happy to help. This would also provide my lion Kenya with a mate at my growing zoo.

My friend Darrell Dettman came along on my trek to Ohio. After more than ten hours of driving, we pulled up a long driveway and were stunned by what we saw. The house was phenomenal, like what you'd expect from a Beverly Hills mansion. We could see they had other exotics—a zebra, giraffes, and llamas—as well as some domestics around the place.

Darrell and I had a good chuckle talking about how these people had money and wanted to pamper the kids, so of course, they got them a lion.

We knocked on the door and were met by the maid. She was the only one home, with the parents at work and the kids at school.

"I'm Bud DeYoung from the DeYoung Family Zoo. We're here to get Nala the lion cub," I said.

The maid's expression changed from a professional greeting to sudden relief. "I'm so glad you're here. I can't keep the house clean with that lion running wild."

She told us how Nala roamed through the house, ripping up the leather furniture, pulling down the curtains, and tearing up the expensive rugs. Most people with house cats experience minor issues like these, but it was exponentially worse with a growing lioness.

The children had adored the lion cub when she was small and lovable. But now Nala looked at the kids like prey, tackling them and playing rough as her limbs and paws grew strong. The siblings didn't find the humor in it anymore. But the kids had wanted a lion.

Darrell and I glanced at each other and hid our smiles.

"Please, please come in," the maid said, waving us inside. "Will you be taking the lion today? Now?"

As I walked inside the house, a six-month-old lion cub, about sixty to seventy pounds, strode down the hall. That lion looked at me and suddenly started running right toward me, then leaped into my arms.

Nala melted my heart then and there. But I knew she wasn't supposed to be a pet. That was lesson number one in raising wild animals: don't forget the *wild* part.

"We can take her now," I said.

I thought the maid might cry with relief. "I'm so glad. You can't imagine what it's been like."

We drove home to Wallace, Michigan, with Nala riding in the back of the Jeep Grand Cherokee as a dog would, peeking between the seats, stretching out in the back, or peering out the window. We received a few double takes from the drivers around us.

African lions are the most loving breed of lions, and Nala was no exception. She was very friendly and would be a wonderful addition to the zoo.

When we reached home, I was excited to introduce Nala to Kenya. We put them together, and immediately they were in love. Nala seemed especially happy to see another lion.

My zoo was still quite small, so I kept the lions in a temporary area by the house while I worked on the bigger habitats.

One day, a man named Emil Doerr came up to my house. He started asking me about the lions and what my plans were for them. I had a one-acre spot chosen for a natural lion habitat.

"What's it going to take to complete it?" Emil asked.

I told him, wondering why he was being so persistent, but I'm pretty open about everything I do.

"Okay, I'll be back in a week, and I'll bring you a check."

I thanked him and watched him leave, thinking, *I'm never going to see that guy again.*

One week later, here comes Emil with a check in his pocket.

Right away, I set to work on the lion's natural habitat.

Over the years, Emil and I became like brothers. He lived in the city but came up regularly to spend time with the animals. I still see him often. He's taken me to pick up animals in other states and offered support in many ways. Emil is just an awesome guy.

Nala and Kenya loved the big lion natural exhibit. The lion habitat was the third largest exhibit, besides the bear and wolf habitats.

For a time, I took Nala out to parades and different events. She was so tame that I took her everywhere. I love to share animals with people of all ages and in different environments. But the more I studied lions and in striving to create a professional private zoo, I stopped bringing Nala into atmospheres that were for domesticated animals.

After the lions turn two or three years old, I don't

come into personal contact with them any longer. They can cause great bodily harm after that, and they need to develop as lions. But thousands of visitors enjoyed Nala over the years. People just loved her, always wanted to see her, and wrote to me afterward to talk about her, even though she had become wild in her habitat.

At about age eighteen, Kenya died of a heart attack. It was a tough loss. Kenya, as you recall, was the cat that popped Becky's water bed and flooded the house. He'd been a beloved part of the DeYoung family and then of the zoo's.

After the loss of Kenya, we bought Nala a new buddy that we still have, an African lion named Samson.

By this time, Nala was getting old as well. Carrie lived with me at the zoo for Nala's last seven years, and in her final days, we knew the time was coming for her to pass.

We were closed on the morning I found Nala. She'd been with me for about nineteen years. I remembered how she'd leaped into my arms the day I brought her home from that mansion in Ohio and how she'd sat so proudly in the Jeep on the drive home. I remembered how much people enjoyed petting her when she was a young lioness and how beloved she'd been even inside her habitat by the visitors to the zoo. My heart broke at the memories, and I hoped Nala knew how much I'd loved her.

The day she died, I dug a hole for Nala in the habitat where she'd spent nearly two decades. She's right where she slept and sunned herself all those years.

BUD DeYOUNG

When the zoo opened again that year, people asked where Nala went. Carrie and I couldn't keep back the tears when we told them she'd passed away.

Our animals are like our family. Some people can't understand that, but those who love animals empathize with how they become such a part of us, our hearts and souls.

Samson, Nala's second husband after Kenya died, had become very attached to her. After I buried Nala, Samson grieved for a long time. He rested right over her grave, not wanting to eat or leave her. Samson barely moved from Nala's grave for two weeks. It broke our hearts all over again.

Nala was one of the first large exotic animals that we rescued from an environment where she had no future. It's sad and sometimes even maddening how clueless people can be when it comes to creatures whether domestic, native, or exotic. While we love to rescue them, it's tragic the sheer number of rescued animals we bring in, and they keep coming.

My childhood desire to share animals with others remains today. There's a kind of magic that comes over people who might have walked into the zoo frowning, but then they're transformed by holding a wolf pup or by watching a tiger rip apart a slab of beef. Animals have a way of reaching in and moving us as nothing else can.

But what I didn't foresee was the need to educate people about the nature of the wild.

One of the most common questions that I'm asked at the zoo is, "Would this particular animal make a good pet?" These aren't the domestic animals but the wildlife.

As the case was for Nala the lioness, people want to make pets out of wild animals. When visitors come to our zoo, I can understand the perception that some of our animals are our pets. They watch us bring the baby animals to the tent for Baby Time and walk a young tiger on a leash. They meet Louie. They see how Wallace comes when I call him. The wolves howl with Carrie's call. She can even kiss the hyenas.

Carrie during Animal Encounters talking to the visitors about our caracal kitten.

BUD DeYOUNG

We raised the majority of the animals at the zoo from the time they were newborns. Most lived for months or years in our house. This creates a social bond, especially with the primates, the bears, and some of the different varieties of large cats. Other than our rescued domestic animals, however, these critters are not our pets.

The news reports of adult wildlife harming humans after years of appearing domesticated make Carrie and me very upset. This has become a subject we work hard to educate people about.

As babies, the critters are cute and cuddly. I completely understand the appeal. But they grow into mature animals with a wild nature. It doesn't matter how tame it was as an infant; animals reach an age, usually at the time of sexual maturity, when their wild instincts fight for dominance.

A creature completely in love with its human master suddenly cares more about a female bear, a female lion, or a female tiger. Then it's a whole different ball game.

Just as teenagers or the elderly go into a different mode, animals experience a transition in their personalities at different ages. For example, there might become food aggression issues, gender attachments, or general confusion by the critter because of various factors. An animal owner may be unaware of this and suddenly gets between the animal and the food, the animal and a mate, the animal and a younger one, or cross the aging animal that has health issues. Often this results in an attack.

There are other concerns beyond the possibility of an animal attacking its human. People up here in the northern climate, and I'm sure all over, find animals in the woods and bring them home. Locally, it's deer they find beside the road or maybe a raccoon or a skunk, especially the babies. But many of these adorable babies can be carriers of a virus or a parasite. Some raccoons carry a worm parasite that is potentially fatal if transferred into a human. Other animals, such as skunks, may be carriers of rabies.

We tell people that if they find a critter in the wild to walk away, call a rehabber, and never assume it is an orphan without seeing a dead parent lying alongside the road. Deer with two fawns sometimes put them in totally different locations to increase their odds of survival. Then a human comes along and messes with Mother Nature's plan.

I tell people all the time it's not the wild ones that hurt you, because you have the knowledge to stay away from a lion, a tiger, a bear. It's the semidomesticated animals, the ones in captivity, that hurt humans because people mistakenly trust that they are tame.

Our experience with animals can be forgotten by people who suddenly fall in love with the animals at the zoo. In some ways, we want this to occur. Carrie and I want our visitors to discover a passion for animals when they come here. We hope they leave with a new respect and understanding of animals that they might normally ignore, such as the hyenas, alligators, and snakes.

BUD DeYOUNG

Yet appreciation and wonder don't make an animal that is wild at heart become a pet. The way we handle the animals can make it look easy. But these animals are our lives. There are always risks, and we pay attention and know the animals inside and out. We take safety precautions that can't be found in a book of rules because we gauge moods, ages, outside forces, and many other factors. And we always keep a healthy respect for every species.

At the DeYoung Family Zoo, we know part of our job is to let the animals become the animals they're meant to be. We move them into large habitats with others of their own kind. Our critters aren't in fear of humans, because of the early bond, but most of them have little contact with us or other people beyond seeing them on the other side of a fenced habitat. We gauge our care by the type and personality of each individual animal and the personality of an individual critter. Yet none are pets.

I mentioned that one of the comments we often hear from visitors is that our animals appear healthy and content in their environment. They get ample food, they aren't under stress, and they're not made to be show animals. These are our favorite comments, because it's our goal to have animals that are happy and healthy as they live out their lives at our zoo.

We always want our visitors to leave the zoo appreciating the animals in a new way while also gaining a healthy respect and renewed passion for animals that should never be pets.

Louie loved rooming with Alysse, and the two of them are still best buds.

CHAPTER TWENTY-SIX
Saving Lost Causes

I adore dogs. Now that's what I call a pet. Nothing can replace or compare to the companionship or loyalty found in a dog.

But Carrie's passion for dogs sometimes outweighs our reality. I'd get so frustrated with her because she'd bring home whole litters of puppies. She'd never say no when people stopped by and asked if we'd take their dogs. If Carrie saw a sign for a dog needing a home, she'd go pick it up.

One winter, Carrie volunteered once a week or every other week at the local animal shelter. This only made it worse. She started bringing home the dogs about to be euthanized and the ones that needed work, had special needs, or were aggressive and had issues. She'd adopt them to save their lives. Soon the shelter would call her about a dog scheduled to be put down, and Carrie would run down there and return with two or three dogs.

One day, I told Carrie that she wasn't going to that shelter again.

She said, "They just called. They have a dog they want me to look at."

I threw up my hands and shouted, "Oh, boy, here we go again."

A few hours later, Carrie drove up, and I saw two big dogs jumping all over the cab of the truck with her. My heart kind of melted at the sight, but I wasn't going to let her know that. I marched out to see what she'd brought home.

The first dog that jumped out was a huge mastiff mix. He was shaking his tail like crazy, and I couldn't help but like him right off. Carrie took him to the kennel and went back for the other dog.

"Just wait till you see this one. I named her Sadie. She is gorgeous," Carrie said, all excited.

"Bring her out and I'll walk her around," I said.

"They were all afraid of her at the shelter," she continued and opened the truck door for this bulldog mix.

Sadie took one look at me and lunged.

I jumped back, and, luckily, Carrie had a firm grip on the leash or that dog would've eaten me.

Sadie growled and fought against the leash like a holy terror, trying to get at me. I think she would've killed me if given the chance. Carrie struggled to hold Sadie and tried to calm her down.

BUD DeYOUNG

"We cannot keep that dog," I told Carrie.

"If I take her back, they'll kill her," she said with a look in her eyes that told me she was not returning the dog.

How does she think this is going to work? I thought. "This dog hates me. There's nothing we can do. Take her back. Take her back now."

Carrie begged to try a few things and asked me to trust her. "Please, I know this dog is going to be a good one. She was such a sweetie, licking my face, and look, she's a brindle, your favorite."

Sadie did have brindle coloring, a coppery pattern similar to a tiger's. She was beautiful. But she was fierce, and I wasn't about to get my throat ripped out by an out-of-control dog at my own house.

Carrie put the terror in the kennel behind a fence where Sadie would be isolated.

Then Carrie returned with her plan. "I'm not going to talk to her. You're going to be the only one to give her food and water. Every chance you get, walk by the kennel and give her a treat."

I sighed. I already had a million things to do each day, and now I had to help train a dog.

"Don't look at her," Carrie added. "Just give her the food, water, and treat and talk nicely. Let's see what happens."

I knew there wasn't a chance that Sadie was leaving us in the near future. Carrie was committed. So I gave in and did what she asked.

I gave Sadie food and water.

She tried to attack me.

Later I went by and gave her a treat.

She growled and went crazy jumping on the kennel in an effort to bite.

That night Carrie told me how Sadie had been locked in a back room of the shelter. She was taking the mastiff mix out when she heard Sadie going nuts. When Carrie asked about her, the people at the shelter said the dog was difficult and they were afraid of her. They had tried to find the dog a home, but she was too aggressive. She was scheduled to be euthanized.

Carrie had decided to take a peek at the dog despite their warnings. Everyone was very nervous about Sadie, and they were reluctant to let Carrie get near her. Carrie said she'd yell if she needed help.

I wanted to roll my eyes hearing this story. It sounded so like Carrie.

Sadie, in her kennel in the back room, immediately started growling and barking when she spotted Carrie.

But Carrie told me, "I knew she was really a chicken and trying to put up a tough girl front."

Carrie slipped a collar around Sadie's neck through the kennel, then she opened the door without looking at the dog and went inside. After a minute of standing there with Sadie, she slipped on a leash and gave Sadie a little pat.

The dog looked up at Carrie and started wagging her tail, licking her lips as if excited that someone had pet her.

Carrie walked out with Sadie on a leash, and all jaws dropped when they saw her.

"Well, I understand her," Carrie said with a shrug when they asked how she'd done it. Then Carrie loaded Sadie and the mastiff into the truck. She drove home thrilled about those two beautiful dogs.

These kinds of stories get to me, of course. So I kept doing what Carrie asked.

It wasn't even a week later, and Sadie and I were completely in love.

When Carrie finally went out to play with Sadie, the dog was friendly toward her, but when I walked up, Sadie was all puppy-dog eyes, tail wagging like crazy. And I felt the same about her.

Sadie and I became best friends. I'm crazy about that dog. She rides in the truck with me almost everywhere I go. Carrie says we're pathetic together.

When I picked up Wallace the hippo in Chicago, Sadie went with me, as she does on every trip I take. She sleeps in the hotel bed right beside me. Sadie gets to go with me more often than Carrie does. Sadie hangs out in my office, and she has her own room, her own bed, and her own food and water. She is absolutely spoiled rotten, just as she should be.

It's probably a good thing that Sadie was so aggressive toward me when Carrie first brought her home. We were forced to bond, and neither of us will be the same. Now I can't imagine life without that dog. That's just the way things seem to turn out in this wild life.

Mountain lion on the prowl. You'll have to look closely in this exhibit as there is a lot of foliage and underbrush for him to hide in.

CHAPTER TWENTY-SEVEN
Animal Swaps and Bud's Birds

After attending her first animal swap, Carrie was hooked. She was captured by the many nuances that I enjoy about them. For instance, the people at the swaps have an incredible knowledge of the animal they specialize in. One person is really good with pigeons; the next person knows everything about turkeys or peacocks; others are experts on rabbits or guinea pigs. Carrie enjoys exploring and talking with the people, sponging up all the information she can gather.

Since that first time with the Lionhead rabbits, Carrie volunteered to be the one to attend the swaps whenever possible, because we can rarely be gone together. Often we have certain animals in mind to meet our goals in building a diverse zoo. But Carrie brings home surprises as well.

When I see Carrie drive up after a swap, I hurry down to the truck. Years ago, she began a tradition of hiding the special critters in the very back. I immediately dig through the cages in search of what she's brought me. It started when she surprised me with rare chickens.

Carrie knows how much I enjoy my chickens. This always surprises visitors. After all, I have so many exciting animals at the zoo. How could I possibly find such enjoyment from chickens? But I do. I love to watch chickens strut around the place, scratching at the ground, clucking, and interacting with each other. Carrie has brought me such a wonderful variety of chickens.

Then one day I found a new surprise hidden far in the back of the truck. Carrie enjoyed watching me dig through the cages like a little kid at Christmas, searching for his present under a pile of gifts. Carrie laughed as I peeled through, passing amazing exotics to find what she'd brought me.

Carrie says people think I'm a big tough guy, but if they really knew me, they'd realize I'm just a big kid at heart. She might have some truth there, because I'll always feel a surge of excitement when I see the new surprise that Carrie brings home.

The new surprise wasn't another exotic chicken; instead, Carrie brought home pigeons.

I'd told Carrie the stories of my pigeons in my younger days and how I'd ride home with a crate on the back of my bike. At age twenty-one, when I moved to Michigan, I took my beloved pigeons to a swap and said good-bye for decades.

 BUD DeYOUNG

Carrie decided to build me a new pigeon collection. I felt that same sensation as I had as a kid. I have a full zoo with all these lions, alligators, bears, and tigers, but I was thrilled to start up with pigeons again.

For quite some time, Carrie brought home all kinds of pigeons. I was so excited about them, and now I have over a hundred beautiful pigeons at the zoo. They live in the old barn behind the house.

Back before the zoo, when I was raising a family, we used that barn to raise pigs, cows, and chickens. My friend Freddy Reidell told me if I ever got rid of the barn, he wouldn't do another thing for me because that old barn was my start. It now has a loft full of pigeons.

Once I had a large pigeon and chicken collection, Carrie surprised me with turkeys. She's always searching for something different. It's such a simple joy and brings me back to my childhood days.

These are the gifts Carrie gives me because she knows they're my favorite. What else could I want? That's how she is, always thinking about me and caring for me. I love that woman like crazy and can't imagine life without her. Even with all our head butting, we're connected in a way that I can't explain. It's easy to get wrapped up in the day-to-day responsibilities and forget about it, but when I look at those chickens, pigeons, or turkeys, I'm reminded both of childhood and of being deeply loved.

BUD DeYOUNG

Top: Rudy arrives at the zoo (fall of 2012, completing Bud's new herd at the zoo with the does from Henes Park).

Bottom: Carrie and I with one of our first white tigers.

Above: Feeding Wallace the hippo a small watermelon with the help of a young man. I always get some fantastic helpers when it's feeding time!

Left: Bud holding the zoo's first black leopard.

Above: Big Cat Feeding with the Siberian tigers.
They get a healthy diet of fresh meat that's butchered daily just for them.

Top: A father and son feeding some of the animals and having fun!

Bottom left: Bud and Carrie spend some time with the baby animals, Pharaoh the caracal and Gavin the baboon.

Bottom right: What the fox say.

Top: A very young Wallace checking out his new habitat.

Bottom: Lions Nala and Samson hanging out together in 2002.

Top: Bud carrying fresh meat for the Big Cat Feeding show.

Above: Bud and Carrie at the lions' enclosure.

Right: A young boy gets to "hold" a young croc.

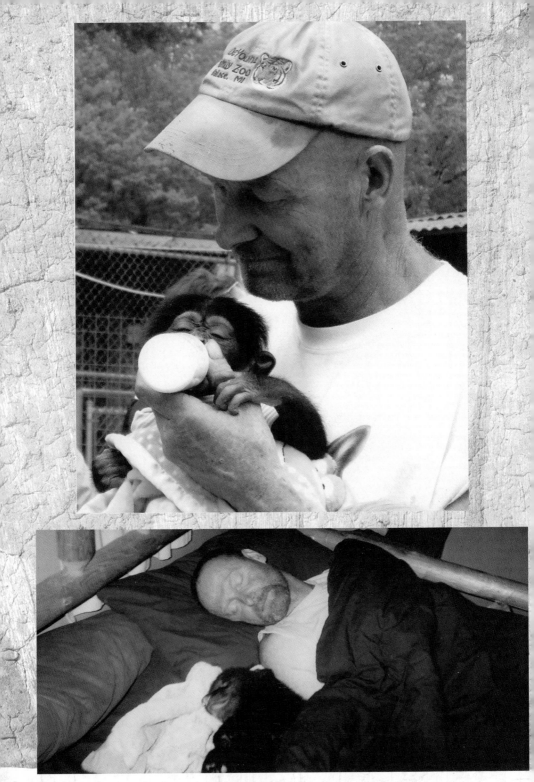

Top: Bud feeding newborn Louie in 2010.

Bottom: Bud and Huggy Bear asleep after a long day in 2004.

CHAPTER TWENTY-EIGHT
The Rescues

The zoo grew rapidly while Carrie and I worked together. In the process, we encountered more needs among the animals in our area. We soon began helping these critters through wildlife and domestic rescue.

Carrie's heart leaned even more toward rehabbing sick, injured, and orphaned animals. I'd been doing some rehabbing for years, but I somewhat put the brakes on it when it overtook the majority of my time. I had made the decision to build a zoo first, not a rehabilitation center for animals. As an individual, I couldn't do a good job at either if I tried to balance both. Now there were two of us, and we could get much more accomplished.

Suddenly, more and more rescued wildlife arrived as word spread that we took them in. We had great opportunities to raise all different types of animals—fawns, skunks, possums.

We enjoyed doing this together, and I was constantly

amazed that Carrie had such a love for animals. I hadn't met anyone as nuts about them as I was. Seeing the passion in her sort of blew me away at times, and I was grateful to share that passion and watch it develop in her.

When friends and family came over to visit, they never knew what they were going to find when they went into our bathroom. The bathroom is the warmest and safest room in the house, the best place to rehabilitate fragile animals. Our volunteers always laugh and tell stories about walking in and finding baby pigs running around. Or once, Carrie was rehabbing a little frog—yes, we even take in amphibians and reptiles—and the frog had gotten out of his cage and was hopping around in there. It nearly scared one of our helpers to death.

We've had squirrels, raccoons—really every type of animal—staying in the bathroom. We often made beds in the tub, where the animal would be safe and isolated from the healthier ones in the house.

After I taught Carrie about rehabbing animals, she took over a good portion of it. She especially liked squirrels and how they like to hide in our pockets. We'd let them out of the cage, and they would run around us, climb up our legs, and sit on our shoulders, chattering and excited for their bottle.

There's something incredible about spending all this time with tiny baby animals, first syringe-feeding them, then bottle-feeding, all the way up to solid foods, then getting ready to let them go free.

We guide them out to the woods and watch them take their first steps in the big outdoors. Their eyes grow big as they see a tree or the wide-open ground, and off they go. They run right up a tree or race into the woods and quickly forget us as they dive into their natural surroundings. At least, this is what happens when rehab is done right. For us, it is a little heartbreaking to watch but also very rewarding to know the critter is returning to its natural world.

Along with wildlife rehab, we began doing more domestic rescue. We get equally excited about our domestic, native, and exotic animals. My dogs, bears, and birds hold a special place in my heart. Carrie adores her dogs, cats, and horses, and she has a special liking for pigs. We also adore cows and our goat. We'll say that this animal is our favorite and then later that another animal is our favorite. Truth is, all the animals are our favorites. They are part of our family.

Once people in the area heard that we took in animals, the news spread like wildfire. People would show up and give us a sad story, and we couldn't turn them away. Other times, they wouldn't even stop to talk. They'd just pull in and drop animals off. We've found goats tied to the front gate, live traps with animals in them, random critters walking around the yard that we've never seen before, and many times we've discovered boxes of abandoned puppies, kittens, and bunnies.

Carrie and I have seen people pull into the yard. We'd think they were coming to the zoo, but instead they'd open their trunks and throw chickens out. Then they'd race back into the car and speed away.

"Did we just experience a drive-by chicken drop?" we'd say to each other in amazement.

It seemed people assumed that if they needed to, they could simply bring an animal to the zoo and Buddy and Carrie would take it. And we did.

We'd also get calls for most any animal-related issue, both wild and domestic, in our area, such as bears roaming around town, a cow loose on the highway, or various animals in people's backyards or garages, stuck underneath the house, and so forth.

Often the animals ended up at the zoo, or we would rehab them and return them to the wild.

As our time became more consumed with rehabbing animals, Carrie continued bringing home rescued dogs like Sadie. She'd pick them up from shelters or from local people who were getting rid of them.

It reached a point that the zoo was taking in more and more domestic critters. We were filling up every available space with them. Carrie has a heart for the sick and injured ones especially. This brought problems beyond just housing and feeding animals, and it began to affect the visitors

BUD DeYOUNG

coming to the zoo to see exotic animals.

Carrie would take in horses that were emaciated and in poor health with their feet in terrible condition. Getting them back to health is not an overnight fix. Hoof care takes a long time if done properly, and it takes a while for an animal to gain weight and return to health after being abused for years.

As long as the recovering animals weren't sick, we mixed some of them in with our healthy ones. People would see them and complain to us or write hate letters saying we were starving and neglecting animals. I guess it didn't cross their minds to wonder why there were only one or two among twenty healthy animals. How could we abuse just one in a bunch?

When people asked, we explained that we had rescued the animal and it would've died otherwise, but they often didn't understand or ask us in person.

More animals kept coming, but it wasn't working out for the zoo. Yet with Carrie, I knew we'd continue rescuing animals. She made it clear there was no choice in the matter. The animals needed us after all.

Still, something had to change.

Piper's Place is one of the few protective shelters in the state of Michigan for abused and neglected animals of all types.

CHAPTER TWENTY-NINE
And They Kept Coming

Change takes time. First, we had to commit to the idea of helping animals but not having it affect the zoo. Then we had to fit this change into our lives. It didn't happen overnight.

In the meantime, the animals didn't stop coming.

We were already overrun with Carrie's rescued critters. But Carrie started doing domestic cat rescue on top of everything else, and because of my complaints, she became sneaky about it.

She'd leave for the shelter with a pile of kennels in the truck. When Carrie got back, she'd set out a couple of kennels so I'd think she had maybe just two cats. But in the truck, she'd have five carriers of cats that I didn't see.

It got to the point that she'd take five kennels, but she'd hide three cats per kennel. I'd come and count the kennels without looking inside and be slightly relieved.

Carrie would say with a shrug, "See? Just five kennels,

like I said."

Later I'd find out she'd brought home fifteen cats instead of the five I assumed were there. This kept happening. At one time, our little barn at the zoo had about thirty-eight cats. And there were many more that Carrie had adopted out.

Carrie also created a program called Piper's Boot Camp, where she takes in people's dogs with issues and puts them through a boot camp to retrain them. The camp includes working with the owners, showing them what the animal needs and how to train their dogs. After boot camp, the dogs return home with their owners.

But with the rescued animals taking over and people continuing to bring them, finally I said, "No more. We can't have visitors to the zoo thinking we're abusing animals."

Yet the need was so great for these critters, and Carrie would not back down, either. We needed a new location.

In 1990 I'd owned a farm a few miles away. I talked to the owner and told him we needed a place to house and heal rescued animals, mainly of the domestic variety. We made an agreement and started renting the farm. Piper's Place was born.

Since Carrie was a child, her nickname has been Piper, or the Pied Piper, because of her love for animals and how she rounds them up and they follow her. At the zoo, there are always goats or ducks or six to eight dogs following her. When she enters a habitat she's surrounded by the hyenas or other exotics because she has such a bond with animals.

BUD DeYOUNG

Piper's Place became Carrie's special home for rescued animals.

The old forty-acre farm included a dilapidated barn, a large pasture with a couple of sectioned-off smaller pastures, and one big area that we enclosed for Carrie's dog runs.

In one pasture, we put sheep, goats, and llamas. Two smaller pastures were used for different types of horses. Carrie also had a stud pen, baby pens, and a birthing pen. There was a round pen for emergency cases and a little sandy arena to exercise the animals during their rehabilitation. Then we had the big pasture, where the healthier horses could run.

Beside the house, we turned an old summer kitchen into our cattery for all the domestic cats. Carrie set up cages just like at the shelters. We decorated it with furniture from the house so we could observe how the cats would adjust to a normal house setting. She devised a plan for the boys to build an outside pen so the cats could go in and out of a window. This fenced-in space had grass and areas the cats could climb or just get fresh air and rest in the sunshine.

We were pretty proud of this first attempt at a rescue, even though everything was old and falling apart. We did our best and made do with what we had available.

Once Piper's Place opened, the animals really poured in. Carrie obtained a license to become a protective shelter for the state. She focused mainly on abused and neglected cases, animals found in hoarding environments, and those with special issues. Our local animal shelter wasn't far away, and they did a good job, so we encouraged people who had dogs that were ready to be adopted or highly adoptable to go there first. Then Carrie took the other cases and gave them the time, training, and TLC before trying to place them in a new home.

Carrie has a passion for seeing animals through the roughest times in their lives and helping them become healthy and happy, often going to a permanent home with owners excited to have them.

Piper's Place was pretty successful. Carrie adopted out a lot of dogs, cats, and horses. We had been doing this for years at the house with dogs, but there was a time when we had over thirty. This was in the summer when we'd adopt out a dog or two or sometimes more in a week as visitors came through the park. People who come to zoos are animal lovers; they tend to have their own animals at home.

I have to give Carrie credit. She found homes for nearly every one of those cats that had been in our barn. The zoo now has only three cats and a few at the rescue ranch. At least that's what she tells me.

The sheer number of animals was shocking, however. I'd shake my head when she'd tell me how many more animals arrived.

"But they all need a home," she'd say.

I've come to think of Carrie as the Mother Teresa of animals. She loves and cares for them with all her heart, and she eventually finds most of them homes. If not, she provides a home with her.

I helped as much as I could, offering advice from my years of raising animals. But Carrie's natural instincts are amazing, and she's learned a great deal in the many years at the zoo.

And we would only continue to grow.

Founder of Piper's Rescue Ranch, Big Cat Carrie holding one of the zoo's tiger cubs.

CHAPTER THIRTY
Saving Bob and Gunther

During the summer of 2010, Carrie got a call from the sheriff's deputy about two horses that needed help. The horses had been neglected, were severely injured, had gunshot wounds, and were abandoned in a junkyard. A warrant had been obtained, and the sheriff's deputy and an animal control officer were going in to remove the animals. The sheriff's deputy asked if he could borrow a horse trailer.

The next morning, the sheriff's deputy and the animal control officer stopped in at Piper's Place to borrow Carrie's trailer. While there, they asked if Carrie would be interested in taking the horses on after they picked them up.

Of course, Carrie agreed.

The zoo was open on that hot July day. Carrie had the usual animal shows at the zoo, so she asked the sheriff to call when they were close to arriving back at the farm and she'd run over from the zoo.

Right after the Big Cat Feeding, Carrie got the call and

off she rushed.

Earlier, she'd prepared for the two horses to be quarantined and given some time alone while they were cleaned up. She used a pen with good shelter from the heat.

As the sheriff's deputy drove the truck and trailer up the long driveway, Carrie caught a horrendous stench that grew more powerful as they got closer. When they opened the trailer door, Carrie held her breath, trying not to get sick.

Inside the trailer, two Clydesdale horses, the breed famous from the Budweiser commercials, stood staring out with large dark eyes. They were tall, sweet horses. But this pair was in terrible shape. Even with their large bones, they appeared small and pathetic. There was nothing to them.

The animal control officer led the horses carefully from the trailer. Out in the full sunlight, their shocking condition only became more pronounced.

As Carrie closed the trailer door so the sheriff's deputy could pull the vehicle out of the paddock, she saw that the entire floor of the trailer was moving. It was completely covered with maggots, pus, and blood.

Carrie called me, and I knew from the tone of her voice that this was serious. We've dealt with every kind of injury and illness, but this was different. She asked if I could have the boys wash down the trailer with the power washer to get it disinfected. I could tell Carrie was shocked by the situation, and I promised to be there as soon as the zoo closed for the day.

Then Carrie shut the gate and turned around to inspect those two gentle giants, as she calls them.

The local vet arrived and walked around the horses, looking them over. Everyone had a somber expression.

"Well, let's get them taken care of," Carrie said, trying to push beyond her disbelief that someone could do this to an animal.

The animal control guy was holding the horses and stopped Carrie in her tracks. "You can see them. We wanted to get them picked up, but it'll be impossible to save these two. There's very little chance for survival. They're suffering."

The vet agreed and also said that he'd shown two other vets pictures of the horses. They all thought the horses should be put down.

On a scale of one to ten, the Clydesdales would be considered a one. They were full of infection, dehydrated, anemic, emaciated, and they had gunshot injuries. Barbed wire was wrapped and imbedded into their legs, and the hairy area around their feet, called feathers, was completely engulfed with maggots. The maggots were housed up inside, eating away at the dead flesh so the wounds weren't able to heal.

One horse's leg had so much pus and infection that it was swollen about five times larger than normal, and the back of his leg was tar black.

No one could ascertain the injury to the other horse,

but it was wounded from its withers (the place where a horse's neck meets his back) to its belly and covered in a thick crust. They didn't know if it was flesh, scabs, or dried pus, but it covered six inches across and several feet long. When they inspected it closer, it appeared four inches thick and smelled like rotting flesh.

The horses stood with heads hung low, but they looked at Carrie, and that was it for her.

"You said there's very little chance. That means there is a chance," Carrie said.

The vet explained to Carrie that it wasn't going to be easy, probably not possible, and the horses would need constant care. "It's going to take a lot of time and a lot of money, and they may never be good for anything."

Carrie touched the nose of one of the horses. "They're here now, so they're mine. I'll take over."

They tried talking Carrie out of it, but she saw something in the horses. She knew they wanted a chance to live.

Later Carrie said, "They just gave me a look that told me we can do this."

Carrie sent the sheriff's deputy, animal control officer, and vet on their way. She recruited her brother, Hayden, and another worker Mike. They had stunned expressions as they stood there with those huge giants full of infection.

"Let's get to work," Carrie said.

At first, the horses were lethargic with the pain. But when Carrie or her helpers tried to walk them, the

  BUD DeYOUNG

horses became jittery. Carrie soothed them, whispering that everything was going to be okay, they were in a safe place, and she'd make sure they got better. She seemed to make a pact with the horses that if they trusted her, they'd improve. Apparently, it calmed them down.

The first horse they addressed was the one with the swollen injury on the back of his leg. He didn't want anyone touching it. Bit by bit, Carrie was able to gently hose off his legs, get the barbed wire from the wound and the maggots out. It took a lot of work, just scrubbing the area.

As Carrie cleaned the horse's leg, she discovered the reason for the black crust. When she applied pressure to the extremely swollen leg, she identified a little hole. The pressure sent a stream of red liquefied pus and maggots out of the hole as if someone had turned on a sink. When she stopped the pressure, the stream stopped. She pushed, and out came the bloody infection.

Carrie kept cleaning and flushing it out and then realized that the blackness was the horse's skin. There was no hair and no life in it. The red areas were muscle that had been eaten away and liquefied. The horse was basically missing the whole back muscle of his leg. It was just dead skin covering bone.

After Carrie cleaned up the horse the best she could, flushing out the wound and scrubbing him all over, she gave him some antibiotics as well as a little water to combat the dehydration.

Often people see a starving animal and immediately offer food, but this can kill it, give it colic, or make it compacted. Many problems can occur if food isn't properly distributed to an emaciated critter. This was one of the worst cases Carrie and I have ever seen, and at that moment, I was busy with our visitors at the zoo. She was on her own.

But Carrie took right to it. Her natural ability is incredible, and by then, she'd had a lot of experience with other animals. Somehow her instincts and knowledge enabled her to do just what was needed.

Once she had that horse settled and doing well, Carrie, Hayden, and Mike moved on to the other horse.

As Carrie looked him over, she began to doubt her resolve that he could be saved. The horse had been shot with a rifle twice, high up on his shoulder. From the withers and down his stomach, a huge crevasse had formed from the wound.

Carrie stood back a moment, trying not to gag from the smell and the sight of it, like something from a horror movie. The once-magnificent animal had declined to bone, skin, and disease. She fought against fury toward the horrible man who had done this to these gentle creatures and against the tears that wanted to burst forth at the sight of the injuries. Carrie knew this horse would take the longest and had the least chance of surviving.

Swallowing her emotions, Carrie knew it was time to

act strong, even if she didn't feel it. Her helpers and the horses were looking to her to solve this.

She named this horse Bob and the other one Gunther. When they started cleaning Bob, Carrie targeted his legs first and worked her way up his body. He was very sensitive. Both sides had some pus and scabbing, but he literally looked like someone had cut him open from the withers down to the belly.

As Carrie cleaned, everything peeled away in thick, rancid layers of caked-on pus. It was drainage that had built up to the point that it was like a river running down his side with huge banks of crusted blood and infected matter. They cleaned him all the way up from his shoulders to his withers.

Bob had five holes in him. One went all the way through his withers while the other holes were across his body. When Carrie bathed him and scrubbed his body, pus came out those holes. She spent a long time flushing him out, pushing different directions to get the pus out, until he was completely flushed clean.

When they finished, Bob looked even more emaciated than when he'd arrived.

Except for the two gunshot wounds, the holes were drainage holes that fissured their way out of his body trying to rid him of the pus. While the gunshot wounds were located high on his withers, the drainage was under his skin throughout the rest of his body. Carrie knew the horse was close to becoming septic, which is usually deadly.

When I saw the horses, I was stunned. Carrie had a look of both resolve and fear. I knew she'd be devastated if they didn't survive, and I didn't see how they could survive. They were in such awful shape.

But hour by hour, day by day, and week by week, Carrie tended to them. She still did the shows at the zoo, her chores, and cared for her other animals. But most of her long, hard hours that summer went to Bob and Gunther. Several times a day, she flushed their wounds. She fed them slowly, medicated them. Just cleaning and bandaging them was a constant routine.

But they lived.

To see Bob and Gunther today, you'd never think that they could have been in that condition, and it brings such anger that someone would have harmed such gorgeous animals.

When people meet Bob and Gunther and hear their story, they can hardly believe it. The horses are fully back to the magnificent creatures they once were. They have some scars, but visitors to the rescue say, "Are they the ones? Are those the Clydesdales?" They're amazed at their recovery.

At this time, Carrie was going through challenges with her family and the farm. Some were situations that were out of her control. But mustering the strength to save Bob and Gunther propelled her to take Piper's Place from a side hobby and push it forward to become a full-scale rescue.

These two horses were perfect examples of how greatly it was needed.

The autumn after Bob and Gunther arrived, Carrie and I tried to buy the farm she used for Piper's Place so that we could have a more permanent facility. The animal rescue was growing, and the survival of Bob and Gunther inspired Carrie to create something more stable with better structures, especially through the harsh winters.

The sale didn't work out, but then I found a ranch available to be leased adjacent to the zoo through the woods. It was eighty acres, with excellent barns, a large indoor arena, numerous fenced pastures, and solid structures. We moved Carrie's rescue in November of that year. It was the best thing that ever happened when Piper's Place became Piper's Rescue Ranch.

Bob and Gunther, grazing in the beautiful fenced pastures, are the poster animals for the rescue. We love their story and hope it prevents animal abuse and helps spread awareness of what is happening to animals all over.

Bob and Gunther will always remain in their forever home at Piper's Rescue Ranch. They never need to worry about being hungry or harmed again. They inspired us to dream bigger than we'd ever imagined. Before, we'd wanted to expand the zoo, then help domestics. Now we were taking on an entire rescue. Bob and Gunther reminded us why.

Sometimes the most incredible miracles come in the form of something seemingly so small.

CHAPTER THIRTY-ONE
The Haitian Priest

Now and again, I get calls from local people asking to bring visitors out for a special tour of the zoo.

Around 2003, a good friend Joe Krygoski called me up with such a request. Joe is a religious man and involved at a church in Menominee. He is also a faithful supporter of the zoo.

Joe wanted to bring out a priest who was visiting his church from Haiti. There were a few special requirements with this visit. The man was immobile and would need to be driven around to see the place. We've accommodated guests with all kinds of disabilities, so this was no problem.

"I can drive him in my rig or the ATV," I suggested.

"No, I'll take care of his transportation," Joe said. "I just wanted your approval to drive him through the property."

"Of course. Bring him on in," I said.

A few days later, as I was working on a fence for the new tiger habitat, I noticed a black limo pull into the driveway.

I was busy, so one of our volunteers swung the gate open and in they drove. As they turned along the roadway, I waved to Joe and his visitor, but I wasn't sure they could see me with the tinted windows rolled up.

After their slow tour around the entire zoo, the limo stopped at the grizzly habitat for quite some time. I jumped to the ground and dusted myself off. As I approached, Joe hopped out and rounded the limo as the window nearest me rolled down. Inside, a large black man sat wearing what I assumed to be native Haitian garb.

"Welcome to the DeYoung Family Zoo," I said after Joe introduced us.

The man beamed. "It is nice to meet you," he said with a hint of a French accent.

"I've got to apologize," I said. "I don't go to church because of how busy my life is."

"Do you believe in God?" he asked.

"Yes, I do."

"Let me hold your hand, my brother," he said, reaching out the window.

When his large hands wrapped around mine, I was stunned by the sudden tingles that shot through my fingers and up my arms. He closed his eyes a moment, then nodded and looked up at me. "My son, don't worry about going to church on Sunday. You take care of these beautiful creatures. That's your service to God. Just keep up your work, and you'll be taken care of."

A jolt of energy swept throughout my entire body. It was so powerful and unexplainable.

The man released my hands, and I stepped back. He nodded, and the window rolled back up. Joe thanked me, then returned to the limo, and they drove away.

Joe and his friend were at the zoo for all of fifteen minutes, but for me that short visit was a blessing that moved me deeply.

Over the years, many fascinating people have visited my little zoo. We've had a Supreme Court judge, famous people, and people in high office. I remember the faces and enjoy their visits. But there was something different about that visit from the Haitian priest. I wish I could remember his name, though it doesn't really matter. I've never had an experience quite like it.

Tigers are important members of the DeYoung Family Zoo and will always hold a special place in my heart.

CHAPTER THIRTY-TWO
New Ideas and Other Zoos

I spent the day at a park in northern Wisconsin near the Canadian border.

Zoo owners Duane and Judy called asking me to dart two of their tigers before moving them into the new tiger habitat they'd completed. I have plenty of experience doing this after our vet's training, so I agreed to help out.

It was eight degrees. I couldn't believe how damn cold it was. But their zoo was phenomenal, especially for a privately owned one. Duane and Judy are working on a giraffe habitat and all kinds of new projects. I felt so proud of what they are doing. It amazed me seeing the new habitats and how developed everything had become.

These two tigers have been at this park for a number of years, but no one had experience with darting big cats. I asked their weight and body fat before choosing the dosage. These factors are important, because something like body fat can counteract the anesthetic.

I gave each 5 cc's and popped them in the butt with my dart gun.

The owners and employees watched nervously.

The tigers became groggy, but I usually underdose an animal and work my way up. I gave them an additional dart each, which accumulated to 6 cc's each, yet they still didn't go down. After another 2 cc's each, both cats finally fell asleep.

We moved the female first. She was the heaviest female tiger I have ever seen. I assumed she must be pure Siberian because she was something like six hundred fifty pounds. We rolled her onto an Army hospital gurney, and it started tearing because she was so heavy.

We covered the tiger's face to ensure the cold didn't cause frostbite on her eyelids and nostrils. We moved her into the transfer crate and got her to the new building. Later when she woke, she was in her new heated den.

When we got back to the male tiger, he was still groggy but not enough to safely be moved. I gave him one more dart. He was a white Bengal tiger and close to seven hundred pounds. Then we moved him.

Before we were done, I gave both tigers 2 cc's of penicillin for the puncture wounds from the darts. I didn't want to risk infection, though there was not much bacteria because it was so cold.

Everyone was ecstatic to move the cats into their new larger habitat. They were grateful that I'd come, but I was glad to help. They're doing a great job with their zoo, so I was pleased to give them a hand.

I stayed around until the tigers woke up before driving the three hours back to Wallace. While hanging out with this couple, I enjoyed hearing them bicker—a lot. I thought Carrie and I were special in that way, but these two were very similar. I noticed how the employees got a kick out of it as well. Perhaps couples that run zoos are like a whole separate exhibit.

On my way home, I stopped at Mary's Place in a town in Wisconsin. Fifteen years ago when I drove a semi, I'd stop at the diner at one or two o'clock in the morning. They had the best breakfasts and pies. So I ordered breakfast at seven in the evening.

As I ate, I thought about my time at this zoo. Such a visit is inspiring to me. I gain more knowledge and ideas from people in the same field when I hear their stories and see their dreams in action. They had different animals at this park, and I enjoyed seeing their methods of construction, the different building materials used, and whatnot. I got some great ideas on slide gate systems and the containment of small animals through the winter. Winter is a big challenge for all our northern zoos, and only workers from parks can truly relate to one another.

I picked up a lot of ideas at Duane and Judy's. They have a state-of-the-art, privately owned park, and they are doing everything perfectly.

It made me excited about our future. I dream about having giraffes, a rhino, and obviously we want to pair up Louie in the next few years. I dream about having help throughout the winter. I have many dreams. The list could go on and on. I'm sure I'll be dreaming until the day I die.

CHAPTER THIRTY-THREE
How It All Comes Back

People help to fuel us through the last months of winter. Our thoughts turn to the visitors who will come this summer and the visitors who have come in years gone by.

I have met such an array of people over the years since I opened the DeYoung Family Zoo. I'm humbled and amazed by the stories they tell me and of how the animals and our zoo have affected them in profound ways.

We've had a variety of visitors, like a team of Germans who made a documentary about our zoo. We've had scientists do studies on our animals. Some collared two of our bears, then watched the movement and studied them for eight hours a day for several weeks to compare their behavior to that of wild bears.

And then we've had average people who are anything but average.

THE MEDALLION

The Haitian priest wasn't the only religious person to speak words of blessings to Carrie and me. Numerous others have come to the park and told us that God has a special place for us because we're taking care of his animals here on earth.

One visitor presented me with a medallion that had been blessed by an important priest. He told me to keep the medallion with me and it would be a blessing in a time of need. He said I'd know when the time was right and what to do.

Through several really rough seasons, I held on to that medallion, and it seemed to help me through. The gift was a blessing to me that I kept in my pocket.

One of our favorite regulars to the zoo is this great father and his tiny daughter, who is suffering from a terminal illness. Whenever they'd visit, the animals responded immediately to the girl. She's just this little thing with a cute meek voice, but she lights up the entire zoo, it seems.

Every year, we'd look forward to seeing these two arrive.

When they did, the father, with his daughter in his arms, would say proudly, "We made it another year. We're still here!"

The little girl would climb into my lap and give me a big hug.

Then Carrie and I would share a special time with her and the animals. Seeing her beam over the new babies or grown animals she'd first seen as babies filled us with excitement.

BUD DeYOUNG

Then one year, we didn't see them.

Carrie and I talked about it, concerned that the worst had happened. Then finally, late in the year, they arrived. It was obvious that the girl wasn't doing well. She was so frail, and her hair was gone from treatments.

The father explained that they hadn't been able to come earlier and this seemed the best day to drive up. We were thrilled to see them, though heartbroken at the thought that this might be the very last time.

Before they left, I reached into my pocket and felt my medallion. I pulled it out and handed it to the little girl.

The words that came to my heart weren't rehearsed or even considered; they just flowed from me. "I thought this medallion was meant for me, and it has helped me out of a rough patch several times. But now I know it's really meant for you. Keep this close to your heart. This is from me to you, and it's important. I know it will help you more than it's helped me."

Carrie and I watched the dad and the little girl leave that day, and we couldn't hold back the tears.

The next spring, we were stunned to see the father coming up to the zoo with his daughter walking beside him. She was healthy and energetic, and her hair was growing back. Both she and her father beamed, filling up the zoo with that light they had always carried. She wasn't healed, but she was doing remarkably better and moving forward. And she continues to rebound since that day.

The medallion was brought to me for a reason, and I

believe it was meant to be passed on to that little girl. Honestly, I don't really know what to make of these moments or miracles or whatever you want to call them. I'm simply amazed by them.

So much of what we do here at the zoo is like that. We do our work, we get our blessings from it, and they're passed on to others, sometimes without us even realizing it.

LOUIE AND THE BOY WHO CANNOT SPEAK

We get many visitors who not only are touched by our animals but touch Carrie's and my lives as well.

Another regular to the zoo is a little boy who's mute. When he comes, he's stuck to Carrie like glue the entire day. He rides on her back, and she takes him everywhere.

One day, Carrie was talking to the boy's mother about Louie. Being a former teacher, Carrie is attuned to Louie's development and intelligence, which is at a similar level to a human preschooler's.

Our decision to seek chimp adoption all those years ago stemmed from the desire to teach people about chimps. Since Louie arrived, this has only increased, and we have great dreams of housing, rescuing, and working with chimpanzees. These remarkable creatures have been portrayed as scary monsters, though this is due most often to human error.

Carrie was explaining this and describing how intelligent Louie is, how he loves iPads and touch screens. For some time now, she's worked with Louie with flash cards and books. Her goal is to get the funding to buy a tablet and have someone create a program out of her flash cards that would allow Louie to communicate with others. The old-school method was to teach chimps sign language. This is possible but also time-consuming, and only others who know sign language would be able to communicate with Louie. People who work with chimps are very excited about technology and the opportunity it affords in creating even better and easier ways to communicate. It's possible that Louie could interact and communicate with anyone.

The boy's mother pulled out a tablet and handed it to her son. He instantly typed out sentences by using pictures on a program for mute and autistic people. Carrie had never used the tablet or the program before, but it was so simple to learn that the two were immediately having a conversation.

When Carrie told me about it, I was thrilled with the idea of getting one for Louie, and I don't much like technology. Louie is extremely intelligent. Sure, he can be a hellion, but he's mostly compassionate and sweet.

Without the conversation with a boy who cannot talk and his mother, we might have missed out on this discovery.

In situations like this, our visitors also influence our lives in profound ways.

I'm excited to see the things that are to come through these encounters.

Newcomers

Carrie and I can pick out first timers when they walk through the gates of the zoo. Some explore the grounds with eyes wide open and childish looks on their faces.

Ours is an unusual park where animals live in natural habitats and appear friendly and outgoing. We continue to hear that our animals seem relaxed and happy. Not only do people get to see our animals in the enclosures, but they are given the chance to get up close to smell, touch, and hold them.

We also have people come to the zoo with cold expressions. Then they start experiencing the zoo, and they look like different people. We'll hear things like, "My family forced me to come here. I don't like zoos in the first place, but I sure didn't want to visit some two-goat zoo in the boondocks. I can't believe I'm in the middle of nowhere, getting to do this."

These people turn to mush when they hold a baby animal. We've had people break down and cry as they bottle-feed a baby tiger or a monkey. They become kids again and gain love and appreciation for animals they've only seen on TV or in pictures in books. They never thought they'd get to spend such moments with these animals.

Often they keep coming back year after year.

OLD FAMILY MEMBERS

Our regular visitors are an important part of what Carrie and I do. Their visits fuel our passion to continue. We may not remember everyone's name, but we always remember the faces.

These people get to see our babies grow from tiny fur balls to adults in their enclosures and even share our sorrow on the days when animals pass away. They come year after year and bring their families, and Carrie and I get to watch their kids grow. We are often shocked and amazed to see the kids growing older and older. Our adult visitors remember our babies growing, and we remember theirs.

THE DIEHARDS

Some of our visitors are die-hard animal lovers. They show us their tattoos of their favorites and tell us about their collections of pictures, paintings, and figurines. They watch everything they can on TV about animals and constantly read about their favorite critters.

Yet even with this passion, most of our visitors have never been up close to many animals besides the usual pet store variety. They never expected to touch, hold, bottle-feed, or walk some of the exotic animals on a leash. It's a distinct honor to witness it. And it's one of the reasons we include this opportunity at our park.

Disabled, Sick, and Elderly Visitors

Other special visitors have been concentration camp survivors, mentally and physically disabled people, autistic people, people struggling with chronic pain and disease, terminally ill people, and also people advanced in age.

We love to have visits from all of them.

We've had visitors who were ninety-eight and over one hundred years old. They act like little kids as we drive them around on the four-wheeler and show them the zoo.

Louie loves elderly people. He picks them out of the crowd and races to them. He climbs into their arms and gives them the biggest hugs, then he stares at their faces as if they are the most amazing people on earth. And in response, they laugh, smile, and cry.

It's incredible the things the animals perceive in people. We love to see how people are affected by our animals.

We've had numerous requests for terminally ill people to spend time alone near the animals. It depends on the animal, but we've allowed some people to go inside the habitats of animals they love. We've also had people make last requests for their ashes to be sprinkled at the park.

Beyond Our Purpose

It is priceless to us to see the amazement on people's faces when they get to touch and hold an animal or when a monkey jumps on their shoulder when they are standing

in a crowd.

Our park is different in that way. When people come, Carrie and I are very up front and outgoing. We enjoy talking to everyone who walks through the gate. Many people say they feel like we're all family because we are so welcoming. Carrie and I make a point of doing this because we simply love people and we want to offer them the chance to engage in the lives of our animals, enjoy themselves, and gain greater love and appreciation for animals all over again.

As we meet people and share our stories and our animals and answer questions, we've been shocked by how that's influenced other people's lives in ways beyond our expectations.

Many times we've received letters or had people return and tell us exactly how we impacted their lives.

I went back to school.

This year, I finally did it. I started my own business after my visit to the zoo.

After I saw the animals at your zoo, I wanted to see them in the wild, so I just got home from traveling to Africa.

These strangers come to our zoo, and we inspire and change their lives forever, not intentionally but simply because we are doing what we're called to do every single day.

After the long months of winter, the people bring the life back to the park. Seeing their faces, hearing what they have to say, and witnessing the joy they have from being at our park and near the animals makes it all matter: the hard work, the tears, the stress, the pain, and the fighting. Our animals make us happy every day, but seeing the impact we have on others also makes it worthwhile.

We are proud to have our park open to all the family members that have come over the years and the new ones we have yet to meet.

CHAPTER THIRTY-FOUR
Beyond Our Dreams

The excitement is like electricity around here as opening day approaches. The cold hangs on in the morning, but my shoulders are warmed by the afternoon sunshine. Through the last patches of snow, I see sprigs of green grass carpeting the earth. The trees reach toward the blue sky, their branches dotted with the tiny buds of summer leaves.

The bears have come from their dens, yawning and sleepy eyed and ready to eat. Before long, we will release all the exotic animals into their outdoor habitats. Wallace already acts ready. Carrie says it's like kids in the classroom hearing the final bell before summer vacation. We're all restless these last days, anxious to race outside, shouting for joy at the start of our summer season.

Besides Dereck and Hayden, more help comes out as the weather warms. We're cleaning up the zoo after winter's pounding. We may bring in some new gravel for the pathways, and each habitat is cleaned, inspected, and prepared for the opening.

Our talks turn again to our ideas and dreams. We grow excited about Carrie's animals at the rescue that have grown strong through the winter and will soon enjoy the open pastures. And we picture the faces of the visitors soon to arrive.

Renewal comes with springtime.

Looking back, I wonder where my life would be if my parents hadn't encouraged my love of animals. What if Dad hadn't let me bring home those little geese or if Mom had insisted her house could have only one cat and one dog? What if I hadn't met George Dragic? Or what if that police officer had shut down my backyard animal collection when the neighbors complained?

If I'd joined the Army and gone to the far reaches of the world, would I be doing this now? Or if I hadn't met Penny Truitt and her family, would I have missed out on having wonderful children and grandchildren?

If Carrie Cramer had never been drawn to the zoo or if she'd moved on after the firewood was thrown into the stove, would the zoo be anything like what it's become? Would I be the man I am today without her? What would have happened to all the animals she has rescued?

And what if Louie's mother had left him in the snow an hour or two longer?

What if . . . ?

BUD DeYOUNG

Such scenarios would have changed the course of my life. My days might be easier if I'd gone down a different route. I'd get a lot more fishing in. I might be sitting on some back porch in the sunshine, drinking a beer, having a barbecue, or just be returning from a vacation to Africa or India, where I'd have simply viewed the wild animals instead of cleaning up their poop.

Yes, life might have been simpler. But what an amazing life I would have missed, and what still waits on the horizon?

I built a zoo on some wooded land in upper Michigan. Many surprises have come along, far beyond what I could envision. I've seen my children grow up, and I've enjoyed sharing the animals with my grandchildren. I found a partner to love and be loved by who shares my rich passion for animals.

People have pursued their passions because I pursued mine.

What is life for if not to do what you were meant to do? I wouldn't be happier with weekend barbecues and yearly vacations while working a job that didn't suit me. I wouldn't trade all my mistakes for the honor of touching the lives of more people and animals than I'll ever know.

It doesn't seem like a choice when I think of it that way. Yet how many people exist without a sense of meaning, never impacting anyone and never impacted by the very life they built? We all should find what makes us come alive.

When passion is ignited and renewed again and

again—as it must be, because life tries to pound it out of us—that's when we see our purpose stretch out far beyond our own sight. It becomes more than just us.

A long time ago, I fell in love with animals . . .

LETTERS FROM OUR VISITORS

Dear Bud and Carrie,

Thank you for letting me feed the tigers. I had fun there. Did Wallace get a friend? I am sorry that you are not on TV. Did the lion eat that day when I came? Write me back.

Sincerely,

Max (age 7)

Bud,

My favorite part was when I held a baby alligator and watched Louie play with the phone. My mom said she wanted to visit in the summer 'cause it's such a great zoo.

Tehya

Bud,

I really appreciate you taking time out of your day to teach us a lot of stuff! I will be back over the summer, so I will see you then!

Emilei

Bud,

Thank you for everything! I really liked how you let us feed the animals. That was very generous.

Erin

Bud,

Thank you for the awesome trip. It was a lot of fun. My favorite animal was Louie the chimp.

Jessi

Bud,

I really liked Maple the goat.

Taylor

Bud,

It was very fun to hold the snakes and see Louie!

Silvia

Bud and Carrie,

This was my fifth time coming to your zoo, and it never gets boring. The coolest thing was when you fed the cats and fed the hippo a watermelon.

Sydney

Dear Carrie,

I love animals just like you. You are nice!!!! My favorite part was meeting you.

Love,
Abby

Dear Bud,

I like you because you save animals. I liked holding the snake. Thank you both. I am glad you were born!

Dear DeYoung Family,

I am sending this money in memory of my older sister, Jean. She passed away a year ago this past Saturday. She had Down syndrome and loved life and all animals. Her favorite was the tiger.

When she visited your zoo, she was so excited to see so many tigers. She was so proud of the pictures we took of her in front of the white tiger. She had many pictures of tigers in her room. She kept all the information she could find about them. I feel this is such an appropriate memorial for her.

Thank you for letting me tell you about my dearly beloved sister. I know she is watching over all of you, as she loved how you took such good care of her favorite animal.

God's peace, love, and joy,

Peg

Bud,

I just wanted to thank you for your special treatment you gave my daughters and me when we visited the zoo in April. We fell in love with you and Carrie in January when we caught the show on Nat Geo WILD. You both are very dedicated to the animals, and your zoo makes a difference to us and all of your visitors. Meeting Wallace and Louie was the highlight of our trip, and I will never forget getting to feed a hippo! You have made new friends who will be returning every year to check in.

Love,
Miranda

Dear Bud and Carrie,

My grandson Michael arrived at your zoo this past Saturday morning a couple of hours before the zoo opened. I was surprised and thrilled when Bud came right out with the monkey Louie crawling all over him. You welcomed my grandson Michael like you knew him. You probably do from all his e-mails and phone calls.

For two days, Michael was treated like a prince. He loved every second of it and has not stopped talking about it, even to take a breath of air. You taught him so much in two days that I cannot believe it. Mostly your kindness to him was unsurpassed. When we left, Bud said, "I love you," to Mike. He will hold that in his heart forever. You couldn't have done a better job of making a young boy's dream come true.

I had reservations about taking him there, 1,000 miles away, and really not knowing what to expect. I couldn't be happier that I did.

Your zoo personifies love of animals and love of people as well.

I thank you with all the thanks I can think of.

May God bless you and your animals.

With love and affection,

Jane

(Michael's Gramma Jane)

Dear Bud and Carrie,

Hi, my name is Michael. I am 12 years old, and I called you guys a couple of times last month. I have a few questions for you two. My first question I have is how is the zoo doing and do you have any baby animals or new arrivals at the zoo? My other one is what are your favorite animals, Bud and Carrie? My other one is could you give me some facts about you two, like how long have you ran the zoo? What are your top ten favorite animals you have at the zoo? And a few more stuff, if you want. Oh, and I'm a boy. And my last thing I have for you is could I maybe do a fund-raiser at my school for your zoo? I would do the fund-raiser next year. Please write back soon.

I live in Buffalo, NY. Oh, and could I have your two opinions 'cause I want to open my own zoo when I'm older.

Sincerely,

Michael

Dear Bud and Carrie,

We are the Weibel family, and this summer we visited with you at your zoo. The wife and I had planned a 25-day road trip across the US, starting from our home in Southern California. We had our 3 kids with us (ages 5, 7, 10), two dogs (Great Dane and golden retriever), and one snake (red-tailed boa constrictor). We ended up traveling through 15 different states, seeing some of the most beautiful parts of the US. When we began our trek, we knew at one point we would be in Wisconsin for a family reunion. Now I'm a big NFL football fan; it was natural for me to want to tour Green Bay's Lambeau Field. I knew from watching your show on Nat Geo WILD that you were located somewhere in Michigan, so I had to look it up to see how close you were, believing Green Bay was the farthest east and north I was planning to go. Our three kids fell in love with your story, and we enjoyed watching your episodes repeatedly (thank goodness for DVRs). For months I had to keep this secret from them, even from the wife, since she can have loose lips when it comes to exciting secrets.

So on the day we drove to your zoo, the wife and I told the kids we were being taken to a Wisconsin cheese museum. They even saw a billboard for your zoo along the highway, so we had to tell them that maybe we could stop by if we had time left over after going to the museum. When we finally arrived, they looked up and saw where we were. It was like Christmas morning!!!!

Now let me tell you, the day we spent at your zoo was by far one of the most inspiring days I've had as a parent. And we owe it all to you two. I understand you get a lot of folks visiting and lots of children coming to your place and that no one child or visitor probably remains in your memory for very long. But my kids had literally one of the best days of their lives because of the way you two treated them and took them under your wings for the day. We call our daughter Madison (10 years old) the animal whisperer because of her love of all animals. Madison made a connection with Carrie that day that she still feels in her heart. Madison is sincere when she periodically tells us she wants to volunteer to help at your zoo when she's old enough. We have no doubt she'll be a veterinarian when she grows up. She's been riding horses for nearly 6 years now (every Saturday consistently, even though we live in a Los Angeles suburb—not too many places to ride around here). I believe the mutual love of horses created the connection between Carrie and Madison that day. My wife, Lori, even "friended" "Big Cat Carrie" on Facebook so that Madison can follow Carrie's adventures.

Now our son Max (7 years old) is the one who found his idol that day. As soon as we walked into your place, we all saw Bud hosing something down, so we stopped so I could point out Bud to Max. Bud immediately came over and began talking to us, especially Max. But you were awesome! After talking for a few minutes, you took Max and told him to stay by your side the entire day, and that's just what he did. Max was on cloud nine driving with you on the ATV, feeding Wallace, taking a dip in the kiddie pool, and generally just following you around and getting the chance to talk to you and help you with the chores, etc. If you remember, you also showed him special attention by singling him out to go with you inside the fence line to feed the big cats (while a couple hundred people stood outside the fence line and watched). It was an amazing experience for him. You also allowed him to walk your baby tiger. I don't recall seeing anyone else get this once-in-a-lifetime opportunity.

Enclosed is a donation we wanted to give. Sorry it took so long. Also enclosed is an RBPD hat and Challenge Coin. I'm a sergeant for the Redondo Beach Police Department here in California. A Challenge Coin is a coin that signifies membership or association with an organization, usually military or law enforcement. The Challenge Coin was given to me by my chief of police after I told him of our visit to your zoo. I expressed to him how great our visit to your zoo was. I talked about it so much that he told me to take the coin and pass it on to Bud to show him thanks.

But the donation, hat, and coin cannot even come close to the thanks that's deserved for our experience at your zoo. Bud and Carrie, you two are more than extraordinary people and should be very proud of the work you have completed and will complete in the future. Again, thank you for everything you did for our family that day. We cannot wait to come back again.

Thank you!

Scott, Lori, Mady, Max, and Jack

I was watching your show this morning while having a really bad day, and I would like to let you know your show really made me smile. I have been dealing with some major health problems the last year and I was having a major pity party for myself, but your show really helped me get out of my funk. I have a seizure disorder and was really surprised to see your tiger Emo (I think that was his name) have a seizure while being fixed. It warmed my heart the way you talked to him while it was going on. I have been having a really hard time adjusting to my seizures and knowing that strong majestic animal was able to get through it helps give me the strength that I can do the same. Thank you for all you do with the animals. It really is amazing.

Sincerely,

Jessica Morin

Dear Bud,

The first time I visited your park many years ago I was very impressed. Your zoo was different from any other I had visited in the past. There was something about your place—be it the way the animals seemed so friendly, relaxed, and happy or just the warm, cozy feeling I got while walking around. I was hooked after my first visit and continued to come back over the next few years. I only met you briefly on that first visit, and that day I never imagined what lay ahead of me and how you would change my life forever.

I came back with friends and never really bumped into you again until one quiet fall day. When I finally had a few moments to talk with you I knew you were a very kind man. You inspired me with your love for animals and people. Your unique way of saying and doing things and your rare outlook on life were refreshing. I have never met another man like you, and I know I never will.

I want to thank you, not only for your commitment to animals, your love for people and children, but also for inspiring me to follow my dreams. I hope you know that I am proud to be in your life, working tirelessly at your side as we continue to strive for the best for our animals. Together we have come so far, but this is only one book in the series of our life. This life we live day in and day out, the roller coaster that it is—nothing can stop our passion for what we do and our love for each other. You continue to inspire me and push me forward, and I can't wait to see what the future holds.

My Caveman, you have lived a crazy and wonderful life. Your story is an inspiration to me and countless others around the world. Thank you for sharing your life with all of us and dedicating yourself to the animals every step of every day . . .

Love always,
Carrie

Keep in touch with us!

TheDeYoungFamilyZoo.com

 twitter.com/bigcatcarrie

facebook.com/BigCatCarrieDeyoung

Let it be known that it is a genuine privilege to commend the dedicated owners, staff, and volunteers of the

DeYoung Family Zoo
in Wallace, Michigan

for their success in building one of the Upper Peninsula's most unique recreation opportunities. The impressive collection of both exotic and domestic animals that they have brought together, the expansive natural habitats that they maintain for their animals, and the continuous efforts that they make to encourage not only recreation but also education concerning the animal world make this an attraction that we take great pride in and help make the Upper Peninsula someplace truly special.

Well into its third decade of operation, the DeYoung Family Zoo, with more than four hundred animals, has distinguished itself as a professionally operated and proactively maintained family attraction. The wide variety of its feline, canine, bear, primate, reptilian, bird, and odd and exotic animal population from multiple continents; the rescue and rehabilitation of wildlife in need; the hands-on educational experiences that it offers to visitors; the expertise that gained it licensing to breed its exotic big cats; and the reputation that spawned its National Geographic television series called *My Life Is a Zoo*: all that and more has established the DeYoung Family Zoo as a jewel in the Upper Peninsula's recreational crown.

In special tribute, therefore, this document is signed and dedicated to honor the **DeYoung Family Zoo**. We applaud the efforts of all those involved in the Zoo's growth and success to this point and we wish them the best of success in the years to come.

Ed McBroom
State Representative, the One Hundred and Eighth District

Tom Casperson
State Senator, the Thirty-Eighth District

Rick Snyder
Governor

MEDALLION
P R E S S

For more information
about other great titles from
Medallion Press, visit

medallionmediagroup.com

Read On Vacation

Medallion Press has created
Read on Vacation for e-book
lovers who read on the go.

See more at:
medallionmediagroup.com/readonvacation

MMG SIDEKICK

Do you love books?

The MMG Sidekick app for the iPad is
your entertainment media companion.
Download it today to get access to
Medallion's entire library of e-books,
including **FREE** e-books every month.
MMG Sidekick is also the only way
to get access to TREEbook™ enhanced
novels with story branching technology!

GREGORY LAMBERSON

THE JULIAN YEAR

Every day, 20 million people are becoming homicidal maniacs.

TREEbook™ enhanced

Available on the
App Store